BROADCASTERS CAN NEGOTIATE ANYTHING

by
Stuart N. Brotman

National Association of
NAB
BROADCASTERS

Poynter Institute for Media Studies
Library

National Association of NAB BROADCASTERS

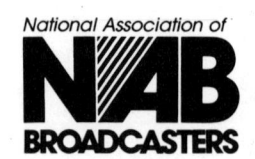

1771 N Street, N.W.
Washington, D.C. 20036
202-429-5376

© Copyright, National Association of Broadcasters, March 1988.

ISBN 0-89324-044-3

Table of Contents

INTRODUCTION 1

NEGOTIATING PRINCIPLES AND PLOYS 3

RADIO AND TELEVISION ADVERTISING SALES
    Radio and Television Advertising Sales: An Overview 7
    Radio and Television Advertising Sales: The Viewpoints of Broadcast Managers 11
    Radio and Television Advertising Sales: The Viewpoints of
        Advertising Agencies and Media Buyers 15
    Radio and Television Advertising Sales: Negotiating Exercise 19
    Radio and Television Advertising Sales: Strategic and Tactical
        Negotiating Considerations 21

RADIO RATINGS SERVICES
    Radio Ratings Services: An Overview 25
    Radio Ratings Services: The Viewpoints of Broadcast Managers 27
    Radio Ratings Services: The Viewpoints of Arbitron and Birch 31
    Radio Ratings Services: Negotiating Exercise 35
    Radio Ratings Services: Strategic and Tactical
        Negotiating Considerations 37

TELEVISION PROGRAMMING SYNDICATION
    Television Programming Syndication: An Overview 41
    Television Programming Syndication: The Viewpoints of Broadcast Managers 45
    Television Programming Syndication: The Viewpoints of Syndicators 49
    Television Programming Syndication: Negotiating Exercise 53
    Television Programming Syndication: Strategic and Tactical
        Negotiating Considerations 55

CONCLUSION 59

APPENDIX A—EFFECTIVE NEGOTIATING STYLES 61
    Negotiating Bibliography 69

APPENDIX B—NEGOTIATION PLANNING, EXECUTION AND REVIEW 71

WORKSHEETS 76

ACKNOWLEDGEMENTS 127

THE AUTHOR 128

Introduction

This is the first book of its kind on negotiation planning, strategies and tactics for radio and television station managers. Only recently has negotiation become recognized as a unique combination of art and science that makes so much in our life happen—or not happen. The beginning of this widespread recognition of the importance of negotiation began in 1980, with the publication of *You Can Negotiate Anything* by Herb Cohen, which today remains the best-selling book on negotation.

The words of Herb Cohen there still ring true, and bear repeating here:

> "Your real world is a giant negotiating table, and like it or not, you're a participant. . . . Negotiation is a field of knowledge and endeavor that focuses on gaining the favor of people from whom we want things . . . We want all sorts of things: prestige, freedom, money, justice, status, love, security, and recognition . . . Traditionally, rewards go to those possessing the greatest talent, dedication, and education. But life has disillusioned those who hold that virtue and hard work will triumph in the end. The 'winners' seem to be people who not only are competent, but also have the ability to 'negotiate' their way to get what they want."

Coincidentally, since the release of Herb Cohen's book, I have been active in negotiating within the radio and television industries, as well as within other communications, information and entertainment businesses. My experiences with broadcast managers in particular has given me an inside look into what powerful and innate negotiators so many of them are in practice.

Part of their success can be explained by their overall job responsibilities as broadcast managers. Negotiation is a large and vital area of concern for someone with managerial responsibility at a radio or television station. Seldom does a workday pass where some matter requiring negotiating skill does not arise. A week in the life of a broadcast manager, for example, may involve:

- Negotiations with advertisers, advertising agencies and time buyers;
- Negotiations with employees and unions;
- Negotiations with program suppliers/networks;
- Negotiations with citizen groups;
- Negotiations with hardware vendors;
- Negotiations with professional service vendors;
- Negotiations with cable television systems;
- Negotiations with a corporate parent;
- Negotiations with research and ratings services;
- Negotiations with joint venture partners; and
- Negotiations with potential station buyers or sellers.

Broadcast managers must negotiate constantly, and they have built up considerable knowledge through experience, including knowledge based upon prior unsuccessful outcomes. The stakes are usually high and the pressure is great, forcing many managers to perform at a higher level than would otherwise be expected. The good news that I can convey is that so many broadcasters are performing ably as negotiators day in and day out, issue by issue. The batting average is far from perfect, but it would make Ted Williams (or Rod Carew, for more contemporary readers) proud.

The less-than-good news is that few managers I have had contact with have the luxury of taking a few steps back to reflect on how they negotiate and how they can refine their negotiation techniques to produce even better results more consistently. That is where this book comes in.

This is a workbook, not a tome that you should allow to gather dust on a bookshelf. It is intended as a resource to improve and evaluate your negotiation performance both generally and in specific situations. It is a tool to help you plan negotiations more systematically, and to help you marshal information that will facilitate mutually satisfactory agreements. Take it on a "test ride" the next time you negotiate in order to see how it can help focus you in ways that time or energy may have prevented in the past.

One of my conditions in undertaking this project (yes, the book itself is the product of several months of negotiation) was that it would highlight the actual experiences—both successful and otherwise—of radio and television station managers, many of whom have come to be regarded within the industry as master negotiators. Regardless of the outcomes of individual negotiations that they discuss here, rest assured that to a person, the individuals interviewed for this book are one very savvy group. I think they are also quite representative of broadcast managers as a whole. They are opinionated, articulate, somewhat argumentative. They tend to pull few, if any, punches. They get results.

In all, edited portions of nearly three dozen detailed in-person and telephone interviews are included in this book. The majority are with radio and television managers from large, medium and small markets. They offer sage advice about how they approach negotiation in general and in specific situations. The balance of the interviews are with some of those who sit on the opposite side of the table. These interviewees provide a rare glimpse of how broadcast managers are perceived outside the industry by the other half of what many describe as a perennial love-hate relationship. Their advice and criticism, while sometimes blunt, is well worth reviewing again and again. In order to encourage candor, all those interviewed spoke on a not-for-attribution basis.

Although this book is intended to provide a broad look at the negotiation process in broadcasting, it has a more specific focus as well—namely, several radio and television concerns that, according to NAB-sponsored research, are among the hottest topics discussed by managers today. The three areas to be covered are 1) radio and television advertising sales; 2) radio ratings services and 3) television programming syndication. At first glance, these areas seem to be cut-and-dried transactions: someone buys, someone sells and may the best price win. But when you scratch beneath the surface, additional levels of complexity are revealed. Although buying and selling involves negotiation in its most basic form, the lowest price doesn't always win because both sides have other needs to be fulfilled. These needs, by the way, can contribute to the bottom line even if they cannot be quantified as easily.

This book is divided into six sections. The first, "Negotiating Principles and Ploys," will help you gain more insight about how others negotiate with you so that you can adapt your behavior accordingly. The issues discussed in this section will be the foundation for the remainder of the book. General principles and recommendations will be presented which, in later sections, will be reinforced by specific examples.

The next three sections introduce the real experts in their own words: your colleagues, radio and television station managers. Each section is organized around a specific negotiating situation. Section two covers "Radio and Television Advertising Sales;" section three covers "Radio Ratings Services;" section four covers "Television Programming Syndication."

The discussion of each of these areas, in turn, is presented in five parts; the first provides an overview so that the reader can look at the area in a more detached manner than one can do while inside the bubble. In other words, I have tried to unscramble the egg as well as possible to reveal how the particular process has developed over time. Next, the perceptions of broadcasters are brought into focus to add a necessary level of complexity and perspective. The focus then shifts to the other side, revealing how those you negotiate with view your strengths and weaknesses. They offer advice as well about how you can achieve more satisfactory outcomes with them.

The fourth part of these sections presents a specially-designed exercise that is designed to focus on common thorny issues that frequently arise. It is a checklist intended to get you thinking about how you would respond. Your responses can then be evaluated in relation to the advice offered by others in the final part. There, a discussion of strategic and tactical negotiation considerations from both broadcasters and from the author is presented.

The final two sections of this book are presented as Appendix A and B, respectively, for ready reference. Appendix A, "Effective Negotiating Styles," blends state-of-the-art thinking about negotiation with some practical suggestions about how to become a better negotiator. Appendix B, "Negotiation Planning, Execution and Review," offers a step-by-step method for planning a negotiation, making strategic and tactical adjustments once it is in progress, and reviewing a negotiation after it has been completed. It includes worksheets that you can use to implement these activities. Feel free to use these worksheets selectively or adapt them to your own needs, such as reviewing them with staff members who are responsible for negotiation activities.

Now you know what awaits you as you turn the pages. Read on, of course. Play with the ideas. Accept some, reject some, modify some. But most of all, continue to stay in touch with your company's needs and yourself.

Negotiating Principles and Ploys

Negotiating Principles

What makes an effective negotiator? Some attributes found to be important include planning skill, the ability to think clearly under stress and an ability to perceive and exploit power. While many other characteristics are common among successful negotiators, these three play very important roles.

Negotiations can be categorized as one of two types: competitive and collaborative. Competitive negotiations are akin to sporting events: one side wins, the other loses. Collaborative negotiations are, in contrast, situations where goals held in common by both sides are pursued (sometimes referred to as win-win).

In almost all negotiations, factors are present that may lead to competitive negotiations. There is almost always a desire to bring home the best deal while hurting your opponent (the other side). A possibly more powerful motive, however, is generally present to engage in collaborative negotiations in recognition of a long-term relationship with the other side and other future parties. Reputations are a valuable form of currency and whether you are negotiating with local advertisers, national ratings companies or program syndicators, your negotiating style, like your station's identity, will become known to a larger audience.

There are steps you can take to facilitate collaborative negotiations. Put simply, you should seek to:
1. Build trust—build on a continuous basis rather than just at the time of a negotiation;
2. Gain commitment—get the support not only of your principal opposing negotiator but also those that influence him/her; and
3. Manage opposition—encourage the sharing of ideas, information, experience and feelings to minimize adversarial conflicts.

These general activities will lead you to establish "win-win" collaborative negotiations. Specific principles in preparing for and participating in actual negotiations are more fully discussed in Appendix A.

As mentioned above, good negotiators typically possess good planning skills. Good planning does not insure successful negotiations, but it drastically improves the odds. Appendix B provides an extensive planning model for all types of negotiations with worksheets that will facilitate that process.

One broadcaster succinctly portrayed the importance of planning in the overall negotiation process.

> "You have to know where you're going. It's like getting to your automobile and heading for the West Coast. How do you get there? Eventually you'll get there. It helps a lot if you sit down and look at the road map and find out what's in the best interests of all parties concerned. Then, through discussion, try to reach that goal."

Most broadcasters are probably planning before they enter any negotiation. Negotiation planning should not be overly burdensome, but should involve the consideration of all issues to be discussed and your station's goals. Another integral part of this planning is to analyze the other side's needs in order to imagine its goals. With those ideas in mind, you can plan for not only the information you need to support your position but also the information needed to counter the other side's position.

Finally, since much negotiation planning involves the collection and assimilation of information, it is important to involve all relevant staff members. All involved should be encouraged to offer suggestions; an added benefit will be higher staff morale.

Negotiating Tactics or Ploys

One area where negotiating has greatly developed is with respect to the use of negotiation tactics or ploys. Negotiating ploys are the variety of time-honored techniques that have been developed to advance your side or counteract the other side during a negotiation. Some are effective in practice, but few are recommended as general courses of action, since they tend to undermine collaborative negotiations. Being aware of these ploys, however, is necessary so that you are not deceived by them. If and when they arise, the most effective technique to diffuse them is to state your perception of the ploy and ask the other side if that is in fact what is happening. Do this in a dispassionate, non-accusatory manner. Once the ploy is identified and placed on the table for all to see, it tends to lose much of its effectiveness.

Keep this in mind when considering whether to use a ploy as well. The chances of being called on it are good, and with enough ploys, you may change the nature of the negotiation so much that it will become difficult, if not impossible, to reach agreement because issues of trust and integrity become dominant. Here are a bakers' dozen of my favorite ploys for your consideration, and suggestions about how best to respond.

SPRINGING THE TRAP: This ploy is designed to entice the other side to commit prematurely to a position on an issue, then use that commitment to trap the person who made it.

Response: The best way to counteract this is to avoid making a commitment on an issue until all the issues are on the table and criteria for making an agreement have been identified. If you nevertheless become trapped on any issue, you can wriggle out by saying that the position you adopted was based on incomplete information or analysis and has been revised to account for subsequent events. Be sure to point out the new information or change in analysis to support this type of explanation. In any event, avoid the temptation to flail or strike back at the other side. Such actions will only serve as an acknowledgment that the trap worked.

DIVIDE AND CONQUER: Here, the other side attempts to create discord between two people on your side. This is an easy ploy since even those on the same side are likely to have differences of opinion.

Response: The best way to counteract this is by taking time out to caucus so that differences can be aired. Sometimes, the other side will raise differences between you and someone else who is not at the table in an attempt to divert your attention. The best way to counteract this is to point out that if there is such a dispute, it is best left to resolution in private, outside the negotiation.

REAL OR FEIGNED ANGER: Anger is a show-stopper and a highly effective way to disrupt an otherwise orderly negotiation. Be aware that most anger in a negotiation is being used with a manipulative purpose in mind. Anger is a powerful means to get you to concede an issue or to put you on the defensive.

Response: The best way to respond to anger is to resist the temptation to raise the stakes by responding in kind. Anger can be diffused quickly if it is met with a sense of calm detachment. The strongest apology you need make is that you are sorry there has been a misunderstanding. Then stop and move on to where the discussion was at before the disruption, or better yet, to an unrelated point that steers the other side back on track.

CHOOSING ALTERNATIVES: Having identified alternatives, the other side asks you to select the one you most prefer. The alternatives being proposed are likely to represent a stacked deck, so that no matter which one you choose, it is bound to be favorable to the other side.

Response: The best way to counteract this is to point out that decisions should be made when all alternatives are on the table. Then point out one or two that would favor your side which have been omitted. That will send a clear message that you are aware of the ploy.

FORCING A FIRST OFFER: There is an old maxim that says the first one who mentions a dollar figure in a negotiation loses. This is because without a frame of reference, the likelihood is that the amount to be estimated will be in the other side's favor. The other side may attempt to draw you out by asking what you are willing to pay or what your selling price is.

Response: The best response to this ploy is to respond with an outrageously low or high amount, respectively. Then indicate that you are open to modifying your estimates once the other relevant issues have been discussed.

BOULWAREISM: Lemuel Boulware was a legendary labor negotiator for General Electric who first popularized this ploy during the late 1940's. During negotiations with unions, Boulware would say he was making a fair and firm offer without holding anything back for later trading or compromising. Such a fixed position is either a bluff or should be taken at face value.

Response: You should request time to evaluate the offer and note that if it is rejected, then the negotiation has ended. The other side may then back off knowing that you may walk away, or will restate the proposition with heels dug in deeper. In that case, you can only evaluate the proposal on its merits. If it is unacceptable, say so when you reject it and express receptivity for the other side to submit a new proposal at an appropriate time.

COURTING: Flattery will get you everywhere. This ploy is intended to soften you up for a later time. Both sides may inadvertently use this ploy by over-emphasizing the importance of personalities during a negotiation. You may find it difficult to resist compliments and warm expressions of camaraderie. Who doesn't?

Response: The best way to deal with courtship is to recognize its time and place in negotiation. If it is still going on after the preliminary stages, it is best to say that you are happy to have developed a good relationship with the other side and look forward to having it continue to build by tackling the real problems at hand.

FAVORS AND LEDGERS: This ploy involves horse-trading, pure and simple. "You do a favor for me and I'll do one for you, so let's keep score." The balance-sheet approach is a poor one because you wind up trading apples for oranges. It also inhibits any discussion of issues since the emphasis is on what you have to trade.

Response: The best way to counteract this is by politely refusing to conduct the negotiation in this manner because negotiations should focus on objective criteria that can be justified on a company-wide basis rather than on your subjective view of what is or isn't a favor.

THE MISSOURI APPROACH: Another old saying is, "I'm from Missouri. Show Me." This expression of the other side's skepticism is intended to convert the issue to a burden of proof matter, and your burden at that. There is no way you can win here since the other side has established itself as judge and jury.

Response: The best way to respond is by pointing out that you are equal partners in a problem-solving negotiation and not adversaries in a courtroom. Any challenge of this nature is obviously one-sided, and therefore inappropriate for further discussion.

CHICKEN: This ploy is a pure contest of threats designed to create an advantage or concession based upon which side can inflict the most pain. Chicken is an irrational game that is about as likely to produce a good negotiation outcome as is Russian Roulette. One's instinct is to fight back.

Response: The better course is to point out that the game is being played, and to indicate that you will not participate in a negotiation if that is the way the other side wishes to proceed.

NEGOTIATING WITHOUT AUTHORITY: This ploy is akin to telling the schoolteacher that you do not have your homework because the dog ate it. There is nothing wrong about negotiating without full authority as long as the other side is aware of it from the outset. The manipulative aspect arises when this is used as a roadblock for further discussion. It may cause your side to be let down or weaken its own position in order to conform to the level of authority that is at the table.

Response: Rather than modify your offer, you should ask the other side to immediately contact the authority who can authorize agreement and to arrange for another meeting once an answer has been received. If the other side comes back and says that the person with full authority cannot approve, request a meeting with the decisionmaker in order to facilitate an agreement. If this is not possible, get the other side to clarify fully its scope of authority. If its authority is insufficient, you should say so and comment that you look forward to a future negotiation when all relevant players can meet together at the same time.

SPLITTING THE DIFFERENCE: This ploy goes back to the Biblical days of Solomon. Here, the other side tries to propose a final settlement when the parties are near agreement. It is often introduced as a convenient way to meet a deadline or otherwise cut short a negotiation. The sentiment may be well placed, but the solution usually falls short. Splitting the difference is not a fair way to reach a settlement, especially if an agreement is near. It negates much, if not all, of the hard work that has taken place to bring both sides to the point of agreement in favor of an arbitrary result.

Response: The best way to counteract this is to point out that this solution, although well-intended, bears no logical relationship to the underlying issues and that the agreement should be based on the objective criteria that you have mutually developed during the course of the negotiation. If time or other external pressures are at issue, deal with them directly rather than have the split-the-difference solution prevail.

RATTLING WITH SILENCE: Silence may be golden, but it also may cause considerable anxiety during a negotiation. There seems to be an instinct to fill the void by speaking, often just to hear words again even if they are not well thought out. This ploy can be subtle and effective because it pressures the other side to talk extensively, perhaps making commitments that would not otherwise be forthcoming.

Response: The best way to counteract this is to accept silence as a form of communication. Silence, for example, can be used to emphasize thoughts. If it continues beyond the point of emphasis, do not hesitate to speak again if you have a point to make. If silence is being used to end discussion of an issue, introduce a new point to break the silence. A third possibility is to inject some humor to get things going again. In all these situations, the best course is not to be rattled by silence to the point of saying something that you otherwise would not mention.

Conclusion

Many of these ploys discussed here may be quite familiar for some might have been tried on you and some you might have tried yourself on others.

Similarly, the principles for collaborative negotiations may seem straightforward and obvious to some. Do not let their simplicity fool you. All readers are encouraged to read Appendix A for future elaboration of these key principles.

We now turn to several critical negotiating situations faced by many broadcasters to bring matters closer to home.

Radio and Television Advertising Sales: An Overview

One daily (perhaps hourly) negotiation faced by all broadcasters is with your clients, the advertisers. Advertising negotiations are the bread and butter of your business. The more you understand where advertisers are coming from, the better the position you will be in when negotiations arise.

Advertising is clearly a major industry in the United States, one that becomes more sophisticated with each new year of growth. This section will sketch out the process of advertising media planning and buying in order to provide some much-needed background information about the institutional concerns and practices that motivate commercial clients and those that work on their behalf. For those who are already familiar with this process, it will be a useful refresher concerning the people you might encounter at the negotiating table.

Development of an Advertising Program

Regardless of size, advertisers for the most part take a managerial approach in developing advertising programs. In other words, advertising is the end result of carefully researched strategies that are typically overseen by the advertising agency and/or its clients.

There is a wide variety of ways that ads are created and then placed in the media. On one extreme there is the owner of a small business who creates, places and pays for its own advertising. On the other extreme is the large corporation that owns many subsidiaries and uses in-house and outside agencies to create and place its advertising.

Most large advertisers prefer to use an advertising agency; however, this does not mean that most decisions about advertising take place at ad agencies. Company presidents and owners are usually interested in their advertising campaigns and often want "final approval" rights over whomever they have made responsible for the advertising process. Usually, sales and marketing personnel are directly involved in advertising plans. They provide input into the development of objectives, strategy and creative elements as well as the media selection. They have control over how much the company spends on advertising programs.

In some smaller companies, the owner is the marketer and the ad manager all in one, and as such, deals with the agency and sometimes the media directly. On the other extreme, larger companies may employ an advertising manager who is part of a larger marketing department.

In either case, the function is the same: the formulation and supervision of an overall advertising program. Advertising managers are responsible for everything that is labeled advertising and sales promotion, even if it is created by an outside agency. These activities include planning and budgeting; coordinating with other departments and other company marketing activities; hiring, firing and maintaining working relationships with advertising agencies; selling advertising ideas and budgets to top-level management; supervising and evaluating the advertising program; and in some cases, handling media planning, buying and evaluation.

Rather than have an ad manager and an advertising department, a non-retail company may establish its own ad agency—an agency within the company whose only client is the company. This is known as an in-house agency. It can be organized to perform the same functions as an outside agency. All aspects of advertising—creative, media, production—can be performed in-house. Some companies, however, prefer to have their in-house agency perform only some aspects of advertising (such as media planning, buying and evaluation), then go to an outside agency for other tasks (e.g., creative and production).

Retail stores in this country generate a tremendous amount of advertising revenue for broadcasters. But retail stores are quite removed in many respects from other marketers, and these differences are reflected in how they organize advertising activities.

Retailers may not employ outside agencies; they may maintain in-house advertising departments instead. These departments are responsible for a larger variety of functions than non-retail ad departments. Additional functions include the actual creation and production of the ad as well as media placement. The reason for this is that retailers need quick turn around time.

In summary, regardless of the type of department or function under which the advertising program falls, all advertisers must perform some basic functions in order to implement advertising programs. These functions include administration, planning, budgeting, coordination with other company departments and perhaps work with outside agency services.

The Advertising Program Approval Process

There are as many variations of the hierarchy of the approval process as there are variations of ways companies organize their advertising functions and departments. Here are some possibilities. Within a company, the ad manager reports to a marketing director. The marketing director, in turn, reports to a vice president, who in turn is responsible to the president. In other cases, the advertising department might fall under the sales manager, who in turn reports to the general sales manager, who usually reports to the president. In still other cases, the ad manager might report directly to the president of the firm or to the vice president of marketing.

Smaller advertising agencies often have a loose organizational structure. That is, the president of the agency may act simultaneously as the main client contact, creative director and administrator. Media use may be planned, negotiated, bought and billed by one person if the agency is very small. On the other hand, the president may be in charge of negotiating the media buy but will leave the number crunching and scheduling to his/her media person.

In larger advertising agencies, the organization is much more formalized and the work is divided by specialization. There are separate departments for each type of function performed; in the largest agencies, each department is further divided into groups and teams according to categories of business and client. For example, there might be a financial services group in which a team consisting of account service people, media planner and buyer, art director, copywriter, and television production person work with a bank client while another such team in that same group works with a stock brokerage client. Each group is headed by a senior person from the account services department.

Each person working on the team is responsible to his/her supervisor within his/her department. For example, the media person is responsible ultimately to the media director and not to the account person on the team. But the person held ultimately responsible for the work produced by the team for the client is the account services person. Therefore, account services people must be familiar with every aspect of a client's advertising program. They are often asked to present to the client the work of other team members. This means that an account services person could maintain approval power of the media schedule and budget without either having developed it or having any contact with the media salespeople.

Media Buyers and The Media Planning Process

Rather than hire a full service agency, one option available to an advertiser is to hire specialized services depending on the need. One of the services is a media buying service that offers the same full range of media planning, negotiating, buying and evaluation functions as a media department in a full-service advertising agency. The main difference is that such a service does not offer creative, research or other advertising services. One of the advantages of hiring a media buying service is to save money, since many do not charge the full 15 percent media commission that has become customary within advertising agencies.

Since media buys typically account for 70 percent to 90 percent of the total ad budget, it has become more important for media planners to stretch their clients' advertising dollars. The goal is to get the most "bang for the buck."

Usually, the media planner begins with a fact-finding meeting with the client and agency account services person. Together, they review all the secondary information available. Then internally, the media planner will meet with other people to discuss strategies and directions that the media plan should take. At this time, if any additional information is needed, especially about the target audience, the media planner will request research.

During this developmental process the areas of concern to the media planner are:

- Product analysis—its functions and intended use;
- Prior marketing and advertising plans used over the last five years;
- Any consumer research that has been conducted over the same period;
- Market potential for the product;
- Media spending history;

- Media strategy history;
- Previous media tests and results;
- Sales trends;
- Competitive data of the same nature as above;
- Comparison of the types of media and media vehicles and their current rates.

More and more advertising data are being gathered and analyzed by computers. For the media planner, this has become more the rule than exception. Research services and computer data bases play an increasingly important role in the media decisionmaking process. Media decisions, for better or worse, tend to be based on formulas. Computers can provide information on the most efficient combination of media vehicles given their ability to deliver certain audience levels. One result of this dynamic is that radio and television salespeople are asked to present their vehicles on the same terms to achieve the desired buy.

After all, the available information has been gathered and analyzed, the media planner will follow certain prescribed steps in order of sequence to arrive at the best possible media plan. These include setting objectives; determining the strategy and media mix; estimating costs and allocating the budget per media type and vehicle; and implementing the plan.

To determine the best possible media strategy, the media planner must understand the target market—how do people use the product and media? In doing so, the media planner must answer these questions (and broadcast managers would be well-advised to always keep these in mind):

- With whom are we trying to communicate?
- Who is the target market?
- Where is it?
- How is it concentrated?
- Is it the same everywhere?
- When should it be reached?
- Is there a particular season in which it is more receptive to the message than another?
- How quickly do we have to communicate with it?
- What is the time span of the media plan?
- How complex is the product and message?
- Does it need to be shown in print or demonstrated on television?

After the actual buy has been made, the media planner must evaluate what was bought to see if the media delivered the audience level as predicted. This evaluation is also presented to the client and might be used in future media analyses as well. The job of the media planner, in short, is to match the target market with the best possible combination of media vehicles in the most efficient way given the constraints of time and money.

Every year, media planners have more media vehicles from which to choose. Media budgets, meanwhile, get tighter and tighter. This means that there is a need for radio and television advertising salespeople to constantly keep abreast of changes in media use. One of the jobs of the media director is to monitor and evaluate change or shifts in media use as well as changes in consumer behavior. Accordingly, this should become one of the jobs of broadcast salespeople as well.

Other functions that might be performed by the media planner or the media department are media billing (making sure that the client is billed the correct amount and that the media commission is taken from the media invoices); recording (filing insertion orders and media contracts); scheduling (making sure that the media receives the ads on time according to their deadlines and closing dates); and verifying (making sure that the ads were placed and were run by the media when and where they should have).

Radio and Television Advertising Sales: The Viewpoints of Broadcast Managers

How do radio and television managers deal with this involved advertising industry? How do they apply the principles of negotiation in their dealings with advertising agencies and the advertisers themselves? How do they direct their sales staffs to obtain the highest rates in collaborative-style negotiation? Below, in their own words, broadcasters provide their insights into advertising negotiations.

I think that every broadcaster that I know of that's out on the street and has a group of people out on the street trying to make money for his company is in negotiation every single day of the week. Not once, but probably 10 or 12 times a day. The major thing in selling today is not talking but listening. I use the philosophy that everybody has two ears and one mouth and they should listen twice as much as they talk.

I feel very strongly that we need to get our people off their duffs and out of this agency syndrome. Get them out talking to retailers and bringing in business. That's happening all over the country right now with visionary managers. They recognize that out there on Main Street there are literally millions, millions of dollars that are going untouched.

My strategy is to know as much as I can about the advertiser, the advertiser's approach to what their marketing problems were and then subsequently find out what areas they were trying to target within any given market that I had the responsibility for.

Try to find out what it is exactly that the customer needs. Then, go back to the station with your people. Sit down and try to come up with an answer to respond to that need. If you can do that, the results will show up in the customer's cash register and you will be a friend forever. You may not get all the business, but you'll get your share if you do that.

I never say anything to an advertising agency executive at a higher level or a client that I wouldn't say to the buyer. I take the buyer and the advertising agency executive to the client's office with me. I never talk out of two sides of my mouth. I think that what has happened is that people will go in and say one thing to an agency and another thing to the client. And that's where you get off the track. Don't be afraid to go to the client and discuss his business. We as broadcasters pay those advertising agencies' commissions. We are the ones who fund them, along with fees that are associated with other services. I don't think that it's appropriate to go into somebody's office and call the baby ugly. Because he doesn't want to hear that. "I'm a jerk because I bought radio X, Y, & Z," that's not the approach. The approach is if the time buyer cannot see the efficacy of your presentation, it seems to me that you have a right to go any place you like to as long as you're consistent and as long as you do not say to the individual client or senior executive something different than you say to the buyer.

We build relationships long before a buy decision is made. We try to let clients know that we can help them out. We spend a lot of time talking with our customers all around and we usually don't have a lot of trouble doing that.

Is there a value that they perceive that they're not getting with the rate we're giving them? What are they hoping to do with the radio schedule? Who are they trying to reach? I like to deal with those issues. I help them clarify these concerns rather than backpedal and try to justify another rate to get them on the radio station.

Too many times, you know, we just want to sell advertising, we don't want to sell merchandise. Our job is to move merchandise off the shelves for the advertiser. And that's basically what we should understand. If you know as much about their marketing and where they sit as far as market shares are concerned, you can have a tremendous edge because the other side feels that you've done your homework and you've got the credibility. They like to do business with you, and will.

The secret to advertising sales is consistency. You've got to be there all the time.

If it's a demographic area where we are very strong and we know that we're on solid ground, why we'll go in very firm. But if we know that it's a demographic that we're not that strong in, we'll have a fallback position.

You may walk out of there sometimes and you may think, "Gee, I hate to sell at this particular rate but under the circumstances that was the best that I could have hoped to do based on the demographic, the parameters of the buy that they were making.

We try to get as much information as we can for our salespeople on the clients that they're calling on.

I deal with account executives. I explain to them in detail how my station functions and how much advertising I put behind my station and why my audience is of a value and why it should cost this much more. That's the battle cry.

If you're out just talking numbers and we're No. 1 in this demographic and that demographic, you've lost—you're not going to win that war. You've got to presell him on the value of the station. And once you've accomplished that you can see, hopefully, you can see through experience which way he's leaning.

People that are close to me think I'm working all the time. And in reality we are. But one of the pleasures is to be able to stop by a client's office or his place of business and go in and shoot the breeze with him about anything and everything, including his business, without any conversation about our business.

Probably the most important thing you've got to do in the eyes of your customers, in my opinion, is in dealing with retailers. Let them know who you are. You have to communicate the fact that you are a professional who's there to help them.

Walk down Main Street. There are advertisers there whose primary goal is to increase their sales and their profit margins. Forget about anything else. Concentrate on taking that jewelry store and using your medium to increase its sales and profits, which we can do. The ultimate benefit is increasing our sales and profits. But the road, the path, is to increase theirs. This is a jewelry store that basically has got six or seven percent share of the marketplace. If you do the research, you know 70 percent of the people in the marketplace do not even know it is in business. And we have the capacity to let 80, 85, 90 percent of the people in the marketplace know that it is in business. "The store has a good product and it would be a good place for you to shop"—that's the message. If we communicate that, if we extend its reach, if we do that at the right time of year, when it's opportune to increase market share, we increase the store's sales. The cost of that increase is cost justifiable. Don't worry about anybody else. They'll be back, they'll be a good advertiser for you. Nobody will take them away.

We have to do more competitive selling. Very few salesmen today know about newspapers, they know nothing about billboards, they know nothing about competitive media.

I really admire the advertising agencies. They've been researching us for 50 years. They know how many cases of soap they're going to move when they buy a 100 gross rating points for four weeks. They really have it down to a science.

The reps are geared to take orders; that's all they're structured for. I'm not criticizing them; that's the way they're geared. But the stations have got to get out and sell themselves.

We've dug the hole. We have to change the sales strategy. We have to change the way we sell time and we have to sell value to the advertiser: return on investment. If a person spends $10,000 with us, we have to show that person how he can get a better than average return on that investment in his products, services and his bottom line. We can do that through media planning. But unless we're prepared to do that, I think we've got a long, tough road ahead for the next several years.

Frankly I've yet to read a media plan that said, "Buy the guy that's number one in news. Or buy the spot on Saturday night because the advertiser's wife likes it." You know, usually a good media plan lays out a certain gross rating point goal over a period of time and looks to maximize reach with proper frequency. I'm convinced that we must make the transition at the local level to sell our product that way and stop selling, "Gosh, you ought to be in our news, we're best."

Radio and Television Advertising Sales: The Viewpoints of Advertising Agencies and Media Buyers

What about the other side? How do the advertising agencies and media buyers view these negotiations? How do they prepare themselves for negotiations with broadcasters? The following quotes will answer these questions, and more, in the words of those on the other side.

It's very difficult on occasion for us to explain to a station manager that our purpose in working out a relationship with that station is not just to deliver cost per point or a cost per thousand to our clients. It is also to create a favorable environment in the schedule such as news and news breaks, or to sponsor a particular program that is in the best needs of the client.

I think there are very few broadcast managers—either radio or television—that have any client or agency experience. There are exceptions.

We encourage station management to meet with our clients. We brief them in all the different aspects of our clients' business that's relevant to our needs. And we find that we get great responses from them when we do this. Very few managers, though, want to get that involved. Most times a general manager is interested in programming and personnel. The general sales manager is looking at balancing local and national sales. A local sales manager is really most interested in inventory control and it's very difficult to find a manager at a station that can really spend the time to find out what a client needs.

I think that a lot of clients as well as station people think that there's a lot more to the process than actually exists because there are many layers working within a traditional advertising agency that they have to penetrate to get to the client's needs. So, I think that they feel that the client is inaccessible and that's not really true. The client welcomes participation from the station's point of view. It is just that the advertising agency rarely solicits that type of communication. So the message becomes that the agency and the advertisers do not have a willingness to sit down in more of a partnership arrangement with a station. In fact, they really would. All of our clients feel that way.

It is very important that the media buyer, or media director, speaks for the client and that the person they're communicating with at the station level can make decisions at that level as well. In a traditional agency, very few media directors can really speak for clients because they don't communicate that closely with them. There's an example of a client in this marketplace right now that reviews all of the major sponsorships and proposals from all of the broadcast stations in the market, and then makes selections from the stations and asks his agency to justify his decisions. Here, the stations communicate directly with the client and then the agency is asked to give backup.

When broadcast managers do well, they listen. If they don't, they are only interested in inventory control. The managers who we find have the closest relationship with us are the managers who are there at the beginning of the negotiation, through it and at the end. They make sure that their station delivers what it promised. Unfortunately, that is not always the case.

Another problem that exists is that the majority of managers feel that they can always sell their time to someone else, that their time is always in demand. For example: "Well yes, we might have promised that to you. Well, we'll give you some bonus spots." That type of approach shows little understanding on their part about the impact of a mistake and trying to deal with it from the standpoint that the buyer has to go to the client and explain why this happened.

A lot of times, I sit with a general manager who doesn't have a clue about what the inventory is like back at the ranch. And when he gets back at the station he finds out that the inventory picture can't possibly deliver what he has already guaranteed.

When I walk into a store, a great salesman would be sure that by the time I walked out I not only got the outfit but I'd have the shoes and everything to go with it. For the most part, broadcast salesmen look only toward selling the outfit. They never think that the whole picture is what will really sell me.

Broadcast managers generally are not adept at changing the pitch while in the midst of the negotiation. Their minds are set on a percentage of the buy. They walk in the door and they'll say, "What percentage of the buy will I get if I lower my rates? What percentage of the buy will I get if I put these programs together in a package?" If two days later the buy changes, they're totally thrown because they might have been heading toward 20 percent and instead wind up getting only five percent.

Very few station managers can make a decision on the spot. They generally have to go back through a process. That's ridiculous.

I think the most important part of any negotiation is that everyone clearly understands what the objectives are going into it.

My advice: before going into an advertising sales negotiation, find out what the client's business is, what he is trying to achieve. A lot of agencies will not divulge that information on their own.

When we have a buyer, we call the station and say "Here's the client, here's the product, here's the demographic, here are the dates, here's what we're looking for." Very, very few times do we get questions back like, "Well, what are you trying to sell here? What are you trying to accomplish? Maybe we could think about something like this." Usually, all we get is what we've asked for. That only signals they don't really care about what the product is. They really only care about selling their spots.

Broadcasters don't understand that they need to market products. You continue to see stations selling their format to an advertiser when it won't work. Probably the most graphic example is selling a classical station as a vehicle for pimple cream—two noncompatible demographics. Stations have not become marketers yet. They do not understand what their clients are trying to accomplish.

If they asked, we'd provide them with anything. We're happy to sit down with them and show them a marketing plan or a media plan.

Stations are under a great deal of pressure for two reasons. Number one, obviously, is a need to meet their budgets. Number two is getting a high unit rate. Those are the kinds of pressures that they—the stations—are faced with. So even though you promise them a healthy budget, if it's not at good unit rates for their inventory, it doesn't do them any good.

I think broadcasters don't realize the kind of pressures that we're under. I don't think that they realize the kind of pressures some of our clients put us under, which always surprises me because the pressures aren't that different from theirs. To us, it always has to be the client who comes out the happiest. I think the stations sometimes just don't think about that.

I think broadcasters are often anxious to make deals. First and foremost, they have to look out for themselves. Everybody else comes second, which is understandable. I just think business could be accomplished better if they had a better understanding of our clients and our clients' products and what we're trying to accomplish other than just to buy spots. Buying spots is easy. You know, selling a product and creating an image is what creates the challenge.

Few and far between is the station that will call and say, "You know, we negotiated 10, it didn't do a 10. Let me give you a bonus." That does happen occasionally, but more often than not we have to initiate the phone call.

You know there are premium positions that you want to be in and you know the more you get from a station, the more you feel like it's really working for you.

Most of the stations will come in with more than you've asked them to, which is fine. I think there's a real give and take. I think that the more you give them, the more they'll bend on their rates—the higher percentage, the higher piece of business. That's good negotiating—that you both end up happy with what you've done in the end.

Radio and Television Advertising Sales: Negotiating Exercise

Now that you have some idea how other broadcasters see advertising negotiations and how advertising agencies and main buyers see that same process, a number of questions on advertising negotiations are presented. These questions will provide the basis in your planning for future negotiations in this area.

This exercise is designed for you to focus on common thorny issues that frequently arise in the course of negotiations with advertisers, advertising agencies and media buyers. It is useful to review these concerns before a negotiation in this area in order to anticipate what your responses would be if these situations arise. It would also be useful to review these responses with your sales staff to reassess your policies, as business changes may warrant.

1. What if your leading advertiser's agency calls to say they are moving a substantial portion of their broadcast buy to a competitor since its last two ratings books have been much better than yours? How do you respond?

2. What if the agency is new, but your relationship with the advertiser itself goes back 20 years? Are you willing to go directly to the advertiser to make your case? If so, how will you do it?

3. What if your relationship with the agency and the advertiser are both solid? If you go directly to the advertiser to make your case, how will you do so without jeopardizing your relationship with the agency?

4. What if the advertiser's billings are average but his prestige in the market helps attract other advertisers? Does this alter your negotiation strategy?

5. Are you willing to make an exception to your rate card in order to keep a valued advertiser? If so, under what circumstances?

6. What information other than numbers can you marshal to support an increase in rates?

7. What happens if the client indicates it is reducing its buy in order to allocate more money to other media, such as newspapers, cable television and outdoor advertising?

8. What if you re-sign the advertiser, only to have a competitor of that advertiser come in with substantially more billings provided it be guaranteed commercial exclusivity among other similar business?

9. What if a disgruntled salesperson makes a "low-ball" offer to an agency, then quits to join a competing station in your market? Do you honor that commitment to the advertiser, who is awaiting a written contract confirming the terms?

10. What if other advertisers hear of a "sweetheart deal" that was made to keep The Big Cheese Company on board and ask you to match it for them? How do you respond?

Radio and Television Advertising Sales: Strategic and Tactical Negotiating Considerations

From the discussion in the previous section, some recommendations in negotiating advertising sales can be provided. Hopefully these suggestions will get you thinking of actions you can take at your station.

Those involved in radio and television advertising sales—certainly those at the top of their form—represent a rich resource of advice on negotiation strategies. They will provide many of the suggested approaches discussed here through comments that should strike at least a familiar chord or two.

1. Communicate your station's position in the market. During the interviews conducted for this book, one manager said, "I'm not sure we all sell the sizzle enough. I know our stations don't. The agencies have forced us into a cost-per-points mentality. Buying on points is the worst thing that's ever happened to our business. We've got to sell community involvement. We've got to sell localism. Selling localism means selling local sports and local involvement and the parades and all those things are the things that can't be measured. You can't put a CPM on those."

Another manager offered this advice: "Spend as little time talking about rates. Stay out of the commodity corner. Don't let people put you into that position. Sell value and service instead. Once you do that rate becomes a secondary consideration. Spend time selling the value of your product. The rest will come."

These comments and others like them point toward the same strategic direction. One important aspect of advertising sales should be your ability to position your station in the market and to maintain that position over time. The concept of positioning was first set forth in the *Positioning: The Battle For Your Mind* by Al Ries and Jack Trout[1]. According to Ries and Trout, "Our extravagant use of communication to solve a host of business and social problems has so jammed our channels that only a tiny fraction of all messages actually gets through." To them, the basic premise of positioning "is not to create something new and different, but to manipulate what's already up there in the mind, to re-tie the connections that already exist."

Positioning involves positioning the product in the mind of the prospect, whether it be a listener, viewer or prospective advertiser. It capitalizes on an ability to look for positions or holes in the marketplace, grabbing them before anyone else does, then digging in your heels to make sure you own those positions. Examples? How about "Avis is only No. 2 in rent-a-cars. We try harder." Or "Seven-Up: The Uncola." Positioning can burn an image into the collective mind of your community, especially advertisers, many of whom are seeking to position their goods or services through your station. They are likely to be receptive to buying your station's identity based on something other than numbers.

Positioning your station properly, however, is only one part of the picture. It is also important to position the role of the salesperson as a working partner with the client, agency and buyer. One manager detailed the merits of this positioning approach as follows:

> "We position ourselves as professional consultants. It takes longer to sell a customer that way. When you run into a customer's store with the bunny under your arm, anybody with a brain at all will realize that the salesperson just came from a sales meeting and the boss said, 'We need $5,000 in extra money and we need it right now.' He's out selling a station benefit as opposed to a customer benefit. It takes longer to sell customer benefits because you have to develop them. The customer first of all has to develop his agenda. What would he like to see happen? And he or she really doesn't know. The customer very often has not thought that far."

2. Challenge the numbers. You can come on strongly with

client and agency/buyer alike by questioning how the numbers you are presented with were developed. Frequently, you will find that there is little basis upon which to justify them, which leaves you in a position to put other numbers on the table. Be sure, of course, that you have done your homework in coming up with these figures, because as an interviewee for this book cautions, "If you really don't know where you are in pricing, you're in big trouble. You'd better know what your property's worth."

3. Be ready to turn down business. Granted, it's tough to leave the table when some money has been offered. But it is far more important for your long-term relationship with the client, and for your relationships with all your advertising clients as well, to communicate that you can only negotiate fairly if you can keep your reputation for trust and integrity intact.

"We will deliver what we say we're going to deliver," says one manager emphatically. "We won't low-ball in order to get the order and offer make-goods because we didn't get them on the air. We want the station's reputation to be one of integrity, whether it's dealing with clients, whether it's dealing with news sources, whether it's dealing with the syndicators, whether it's dealing with our employees. That gets articulated in the course of a negotiation. For example, we don't go out with outrageous estimates on what a program will deliver for you. We go out with realistic estimates. In other words, we want to be believable and the only way you can be believable is to prove over the long term that what you say is believable. That's part of our overall integrity goal."

Perhaps the most visible sign of your integrity in advertising sales is your rate card. Rate cards should be developed carefully and modified across-the-board only when market conditions warrant. You should be prepared to discuss the process of developing the rate card with the other side. Beyond that, don't get suckered into abandoning your rate card for some other deal. If the rate card has been developed to reflect reasonable criteria, it can and should be used as a powerful negotiation tool.

"The thing that we decided," said one manager, "was that we were going to have total and absolute integrity on our rate card. I was in a little town with a store that was having a 'Going Out of Business' sale. They call us up. We're brand new in the radio business. They ask me to come over. And I go over there and start talking to them. The bottom line is this. The store owner says, 'I am going to pay you cash in advance and I want my rates discounted 50 percent.'' I said, 'I'm sorry our rate cards are rate cards and that's it.' He said, 'Listen. This place is going out of business. In four days, the doors close. We're leaving town. All I want from you is spots right now, inventory that is not being used. I'm going to pay you cash right now, upfront. Do it. ' The guy's trying to sell me. And I'm saying integrity on a rate card is more important. I'm not going to do it. So I said to him, 'I'll tell you what, I am leaving, I'm not going to deal with you.' He said, 'Fine, go ahead, you're just losing cash.' And I walked out the door and I thought to myself, 'There went $200 or whatever it was, right down the tubes.' So I turned around and went back in and said, 'I'll make you a deal.' 'Yes,' he said, 'now you're talking, I knew you would—money talks.' I said, 'You're right. I am going to do this for you. I am going to sell you my 15-second spots at half the price.' He says, 'Well, that sounds good.' I gave it to him for half price and then I told him, 'The only deal you have to do with me, you have to let me run them back to back. Four of them, back to back.' The bottom line, I told him, was that he wanted them for half price. I said I'd do it, but I had to run four of them back to back. That made it a minute spot. But he was actually paying more for that minute spot than if he'd have bought them off the rate card. He saw what I was doing, and he finally gave in and bought my spots at my rates. And he paid me cash in advance."

Sticking by your rate card, however, does not mean that you should not develop alternative plans based on it. Remember, the name of the game is to generate as many options as possible.

"I put together plans made off my rate card: plans I feel that will work for the client. I go in with three plans and I still argue with myself whether I should list the least expensive first or last and after all the years I've been doing this, I can't really tell you which one works best. I'll go in and pitch him the top bracket. If he can't buy that, then I suggest perhaps he buy this and if he cannot buy that, I generally will have a third position and accept that."

And don't forget the powerful impact that a sense of humor can have.

"I went to a major advertiser who had been on our radio station using morning drive only. And the preamble to all this was, 'Don't you touch my rates. I've been with you a long time. I don't want a rate increase. I won't stand for it. I'll cancel.' This went on for weeks. So the day came that I had to go down to see him, and I went with a salesman. We walked into his office, sat down, and I wrote down three numbers—one number where he currently was, another number where I wanted him to be realistically on the rate increase and a third number that was a compromise between the two numbers. And then I pulled a deck of cards out of my pocket, and we then cut the deck for the high rate and the low rate, and if he beat me on the draw he would have gotten the low rate for six months. I won the draw. He would pay me the high rate. I gave him the middle rate.''

4. Delegate negotiating authority properly. You cannot be at every advertising negotiation. You have to rely on your staff to conduct the vast majority. So you must be able to rely on their judgment. As a result, you should continuously discuss station policy with your staff. But you must give them enough authority to negotiate properly as well.

As one manager commented:

''I'm the boss and I go out with my salesman and we establish that he's going to make the pitch. What I do is I just answer questions and give him support. And very rarely will I add anything unless I'm asked to, unless I see something that was missed and is obvious. I just keep my mouth shut other than that. If I'm going to make the pitch, it's because my salesman has a tough time with this client. I make the presentation but I always bring my salesman in with me and get his assurance in regard to the particular benefits in any event.''

5. Establish a mutual sales agenda. Prior to collaborative-style negotiations, it is important that planning takes place. One aspect of planning is for both sides to think ahead about what the other side feels are important topics to discuss.

''Before we go in we've already gotten some of the ground rules laid out to us in advance: that the buy is coming up and we're going in now to negotiate that buy. So, for example, we'll know basically how many rating points a week they're going to buy for the market. We know whether it's a 30-second spot or a 60-second spot. We know whether they're going to buy just Monday through Friday. All those parameters are laid out by the buyer before we get in there. So, we can do our homework before we go in and we don't take too much of his time or more time than we need because we have other things to do. We have other calls to make.''

6. Keep your eye on the ball. It is easy to be distracted by outside forces from focusing on what you want to achieve in a negotiation. Therefore, it is important to focus continually on what outcomes will be acceptable to you. In the words of one broadcast manager:

''As I'm driving to the pitch or presentation, I always say, 'What is our goal? What do we want to walk away with?' I always know what my goal is, what I will have wanted to achieve, at the conclusion of that meeting.''

7. Keep the other side engaged. Negotiation is a highly interactive process. It is important to maintain momentum by continually focusing the other side's attention on the various issues for which agreement is sought.

''Basically, what I look for is agreement. I like to try and get the client to agree with me on anything. If they start to agree on what their targets are, for their client, a negotiating trail or a trail of agreement begins.''

''If anybody comes back with another offer, that means you're on your way to a close. You know, when they say they love it and they sign right here, then we immediately talk about golf or something. One of the biggest problems, by the way, with most salespeople is that they tend to buy back the deal they just made. They get the ardor, then they want to keep talking about how wonderful it is.''

8. Be sensitive to the mood of the negotiation. Listening during a negotiation requires more than hearing what the other side is saying. Every negotiation has its own mood, and you should try to tune in to it in order to understand what the words really mean.

''There's just a whole mood that seems to all of a sudden go boom. Everybody is in a position where instead of acting as adversaries toward each other, all of a sudden now you're working together to 'when we start this,' or 'when we get this on the air.' You're talking about what we're going to do together. All of a sudden the adversarial part of it seems to disappear.''

''You have to anticipate when it's time to stop the shadowboxing and when it s time to go in and say, 'We want to have you along and we're ready for you to make a commitment to us.''

9. React to surprises by caucusing. One major rule to keep in mind is not to respond quickly to surprises during a negotiation. If an issue arises that you need advice from others on your staff, feel free to stop and discuss that issue with them away from the table.

''Let's say the negotiation is to buy time on your station and suddenly they say, 'Now, you understand 50 percent has to be in prime time.' You had no way of knowing; in all of your planning, you never figured on that. That throws you totally off base. You should say, 'Now wait a minute, that changes the game.' And if they say, 'Well, your competition was able to redo it on that basis easily,' and you know you can't, then you've got to take time out to see what you can do."

10. Be ready to close at any time. Timing may not be everything, but it certainly makes a difference in many advertising sales negotiations. The best broadcast sellers are adroit enough to roll with the punches rather than plod along mechanically through a pre-planned selling sequence. In short, when you spot your best shot at closing, go for it.

"My biggest surprise was when I went into a client — a very difficult client I might add — that was on the air, then cancelled and wasn't on the air for quite a while. I went in there and I pitched him plan one, plan two, plan three. It was all on one piece of paper. And when I got done he said, 'I'll take it.' And I looked at him and I realized he took the whole damn thing. Plan one had the stand-alone, plan two had its own terms plus a little of plan one and plan three had parts of plan one and plan two with additions. He took the whole damn thing. So I quickly in my mind realized what was going on. I said, 'Okay, I'll put it into a contract and I'll be back in a half hour and we'll get started on this thing.' "

Conclusion

These 10 suggestions should be the foundation for your own policies on sales negotiations. By completing the exercises you should already have begun re-evaluating your station's style of advertiser negotiations. Hopefully, changes in that style will only be minor. Since these recommendations came from discussions with broadcasters, many may already be in place.

---

[1] Al Reis and Jack Trout, *Marketing Warfare,* (New York: McGraw-Hill, 1986).

Radio Ratings Services: An Overview

Another set of negotiations faced by many broadcasters is with radio ratings service companies. While not as frequent as negotiations with advertisers, these negotiations are important and careful attention to planning including an appraisal of the other side is recommended. Some background biographical information concerning radio ratings services is provided below to assist your planning activities.

The Growth of Arbitron

James Seiler formed the American Research Bureau (ARB) in 1949 to initiate a syndicated television ratings service. The ARB had begun radio experiments by the time he departed as president in 1964 in order to capitalize on a perceived market opportunity to launch a local market radio service using open-ended personal radio diaries. Instead of receiving a household diary for each set, each person in the household received an individual diary. These were open-ended diaries with a page for each day of the week; the listener-respondent filled it in as he or she listened, whether in or out of home. By 1967, this methodology was refined to the point where a syndicated service utilizing individual radio diaries was launched by ARB.

The ARB Radio Local Market Service subsequently was accredited by the Broadcast Rating Council in 1968. It began to demonstrate slow but steady acceptance in competition with Pulse, the then-industry leader. Pulse capitalized on the perceived weakness of the Hooper local radio audience measurement service, which had achieved its market leadership before World War II. Hooper had been supported by the radio networks, which sought data that could be brought to advertising agencies for time sales. Network researchers were convinced that the Hooper methodology of telephone coincidental interviews was the most accurate and valid measurement tool. Over time, however, deficiencies in this methodology became apparent. The Hooper service was limited to radio sets in use and excluded prime-time dayparts to avoid a comparison with television viewing. Telephone interviews tended to underestimate radio audiences because the telephone sample was heavily skewed in favor of those who owned television sets as well. Additionally, since a sizeable number of American homes did not have telephones, the samples were not fully representation.

In 1973, American Research Bureau changed its name to Arbitron. In 1982, Arbitron changed its corporate name, to The Arbitron Ratings Company in order to position itself more clearly with those it sought out as diary respondents.

When Arbitron replaced its monthly surveys with quarterly ones in all radio markets, its prime objective was to spread interviewing over three months and thus produce a more representative report. The opportunity and incentive for special promotions and programming to hype ratings thus could be materially reduced, as could the effect of unusual weather and local events. In 1984, Arbitron inaugurated its Arbitrends System in all continuously measured markets. Arbitrends utilizes a station's IBM-XT or compatible computer to deliver Arbitron report data. Arbitron completes the averaging, trending, and analysis that a station needs, before the books are printed, which makes possible a rolling average report that combines the most recent three months. The station subscriber can select the data which is most useful, then have it downloaded from Arbitron's computer to the station's computer.

The Growth of Birch

In 1975, Thomas Birch began experimenting with tracking weekly market shares for the Storz stations between Arbitron reports. In 1979, Birch launched a competing radio ratings service: Birch Radio.

The Birch technique utilizes a telephone interview to obtain by recall the listening activity of one designated person per sample household for the past 24 hours. This is in contrast to the telephone coincidental technique employed by Hooper and Pulse. The Birch interviewer probes for start and stop times, location, and station heard for each listening period during the previous day. Dayparts are from 5:00 A.M.—10:00 A.M.

and 10:00 A.M.—3:00 P.M., and from 7:00 P.M.—midnight the previous night, and from 3:00 P.M.—7:00 P.M.

Birch uses several stages to arrive at its sample. First, phone numbers are selected from the A.C. Nielsen Total Telephone Frame for the survey area, sorted by county. Second, a review process is conducted in order to bring nonlisted telephone households into the sample. Finally, the interviewer utilizes a random sampling technique that selects the family member to interview in order to improve statistical representativeness.

The Birch quarterly reports cover average quarter-hour, daily, and weekly cumes by dayparts and demographic graphs in addition to location of listening and limited product usage results. Birch believes its data is more comprehensive than Arbitron's and ensures speedier delivery in hard-copy format.

Two often-articulated criticisms of Birch's unaided telephone recall interview methodology are that it can produce faulty information by respondents who are asked to recall listening patterns on the spot, and that there are a significant number of unanswered telephone numbers produced by the original sample selection.

Birch emphasizes factors such as its method's accurate, low-cost, monthly data, high reponse rate, two-week delivery, and qualitative data covering 20 product and service categories over an interviewing period of three months. Additionally, in an effort to answer a major complaint from advertising agencies and broadcasters alike—namely, that Birch's telephone interviews of respondents were not being adequately monitored by supervisors for consistency—the company now rents three central WATS telephone calling facilities in Sarasota and Coral Springs, Florida and San Antonio, Texas which facilitated more supervision. Birch is also scheduled to open two facilities in 1988. Additionally, it has entered into a "cooperative arrangement" with A.C. Nielsen Company that provides for the two companies to join forces on several projects, including marketing both radio and television audience information to local agencies and advertisers. Birch Radio's quantitative and qualitative data also is scheduled to be available on Nielsen's computerized "Spot Buyer" media planning and evaluation system.

An important element of Birch's growing success, according to executives at the firm, has been the acceptance of its methodology and qualitative data among advertising agencies. This acceptance, in turn, has caused some broadcasters to take a closer look at the service, either as a complement or alternative to Arbitron.

Arbitron and Birch: Competitive Considerations

Arbitron and Birch must continually fight for methodology acceptance among advertising agencies, radio executives and the research community. One of Birch's contentions in soliciting clients is that its telephone methodology has a higher response rate—about 55-60 percent—than Arbitron's diary system, which has been delivering around a 40 percent response rate.

In order to alleviate its response rate problem, Arbitron began offering higher, though still nominal, financial incentives to diary keepers during its Fall 1986 survey. An additional $1.00 premium per household is now offered. This plan seems to be working; the average total survey area response rate has climbed from 40 percent to 44.7 percent since its inception. Moreover, Arbitron has moved to bolster the response for 18- to 24-year-old males; Arbitron began sending a $2.00 premium to each person 12 and older in a survey household with an 18- to 24-year-old male.

Overall, Arbitron still retains the advantage of established acceptance among advertising agencies and independent media time-buying companies. Birch, however, claims to influence 40 percent of the national radio advertising expenditures. A major concern of radio station managers is Arbitron's rates. Arbitron has been encountering resistance from broadcasters on renewing contracts, and has gradually been taking some steps to make its overall pricing structure more attractive.

Beyond Ratings

Price is an important part of the decision to subscribe to a ratings service, but it should not be viewed as the only one.

Ratings, regardless of cost, can never show how effectively a station communicates with its audience, nor can they show the rapport and trust a station has with its audience. Ratings may be necessary to sell some advertisers, but good salespeople will use ratings as a starting point and communicate a station's qualities in other ways besides reference to audience numbers.

Despite their importance, there is a world beyond radio ratings. Broadcast managers who keep this in mind can both increase their advertising rates and negotiate with Arbitron and Birch armed with a broader perspective of the area as a whole.

Radio Ratings Services: The Viewpoints of Broadcast Managers

How do broadcasters deal with these firms? How do they confront the market power enjoyed by Arbitron? How do they deal with Birch, a relatively newer firm? In the following quotes, broadcasters offer their views on these and other subjects.

My problem in dealing with Arbitron, specifically, has been a lack of resilience from the standpoint of their rates. I think their costs are out of line with the service they provide and they are unwilling to modify or negotiate from a rate standpoint.

We have gone through books where we have not subscribed, for instance, when Arbitron introduced the winter book into the market. We basically did not subscribe for a year to that and went through two periods where we were not providing data from the winter book. It really had very little, if any, effect upon our sales revenue.

Arbitron became very arbitrary and very expensive. I just called them and cancelled. They don't need the money. They really are not interested in smaller-sized markets.

For a market of my size, the rate is prohibitive; therefore, I did not renew this year for the first time in many, many years.

I find the way to sell radio today is our performance. You can have a number-one rating and not sell the product, so where the hell are you? You live by the ratings, you die by the ratings. I say pass. Our business is very healthy.

We're in an unmeasured market. Once every three years, the nationwide county-by-county sweep, of course, comes through. It's kind of an interesting thing because we have accounts, retail accounts, who use the argument, "Well, show me the book." And that's a put-off on their part. They don't know how to read the book any better than I do.

The local advertiser really doesn't care, he doesn't care about numbers at all. We sell them on the benefits of the radio station and the fact that we are trying to generate results for him. Numbers don't mean a thing.

I believe that the biggest problem with Arbitron is that it's overkill. There's so much information that's within each book that is not used. Just sell me a raw basic book of all major dayparts. As far as I'm concerned, they can eliminate the total survey area and just go down to metro only, because 99 percent of the buys made during the day are made on metro.

My thinking about Arbitron is that at this point, more or less, they offer a necessary commodity. I deal with them on that basis. I think if we can get an Arbitron at a fairly good rate, I think all of our people would like to have it. It has become a necessary evil regarding a pretty large percentage of our business. And when so much of our revenue is national, which uses more often than not the Arbitron ratings, it's important for us to have some rating service. I think it's a good service. I don't think I'd feel real comfortable without it, although I think we could go on without it. We feel more comfortable having it than not having it. But I don't think any of us would be afraid not to have Arbitron.

Arbitron is the one we subscribe to. We don't subscribe to Birch for the plain and simple reason that Birch does not have the acceptance of the advertising community—the ones who really make the advertising buys. And I can say that with pretty good knowledge, because at this radio station I oversee all of the national advertising buys. I make direct calls upon the agencies, the buyers, the planners and so forth. And I also have a very good strong input through my local sales management and salesmen. So now we're stuck with Arbitron and that, I think, has been one of the main problems with Arbitron's pricing. They're the only game in town. For our side of the business—the radio side—they really amount to a monopoly. So it's kind of difficult based on the fact that they're really the only game in town that we have trouble with their pricing.

If you have an alternative, then you can make some headway with them. If you don't have an alternative, you have to play their game. Our alternative is Birch, which will be surveying the market twice a year. We'll get along fine without Arbitron.

My view is a minority view in radio broadcasting having to do with Arbitron. I think they've probably got a pretty good product. My problem is its misuse. That's something that has to do with the buyer, not with the seller of the data. The problem is that both data, Arbitron and Birch, are misused by the buying community. Buying a radio station's audience on a cost-per-point basis is ludicrous. I don't know a 25-year-old who's like a 54-year-old.

Radio Ratings Services: The Viewpoints of Arbitron and Birch

How do the ratings services firms themselves see the negotiation? What are they looking for when they come to the table? How do they view the product they sell to the industry? Below are those views from the two leading radio rating services companies.

Arbitron Viewpoints

I think the negotiation that broadcasters are talking about is primarily one of price. Because of the relationship we have with the industry, we're not able to move around in that area. Does it mean that you can't look at Arbitron and talk about the things you want your service to do and discuss how it is? No. We view negotiation to be really an ongoing process. It's about service. In fact, broadcasters have many ways to negotiate with Arbitron. They are negotiating with Arbitron and probably don't even know it. They negotiate through the NAB's committee (COLRAM—the Committee on Local Radio Audience Measurement) dealing with radio research. They negotiate through the Electronic Media Rating Council, which sets standards for Arbitron. They negotiate through the Arbitron Radio Advisory Council, which certainly has power over Arbitron. The Advisory Council acts as an ombudsman and makes suggestions to us about the enhancements of our service. The Advisory Council also is a good springboard for us—we cast ideas out on them: "There's an idea we think we want to do, what do you think?" So we get back some good advice. There's a constant negotiating process going on. As to individual stations, occasionally there are some precise individual needs that we at least take a look at. It depends on how it's presented to us.

At this point, what I hear back from broadcasters is that they want something that is accepted by the advertising agencies. If it's accepted by the agencies, they'll buy it, because that's what they're buying the information for—primarily as a sales tool and secondarily as a programming tool.

A broadcaster friend told me, "When I originally bought Arbitron, I thought I was buying a book, sending you a check. Then what I found out was that when I got Arbitron I really got a service, because our account executive went in and worked with the station's sales staff to better understand it." He said that every time the Arbitron rep came in, his billings went up the next month. He said it was just a matter of the sales staff being enthused about being able to understand more about their station in the marketplace." He said, "So now I understand that I got a lot more than a book." Not many broadcasters recognize that fact.

I'm sure in some quarters there's fear. Some of it is the fear of the unknown because they have failed to study what Arbitron does for them. There is the fact that what we do at Arbitron is like a report card. You look at that report card, by God, and that's your future in your hand. In that sense, any ratings company is going to have that kind of a fear factor built into it.

If I were a broadcaster, I would want to, first of all, make sure that I am dealing with a quality service: am I being brought up to date on any changes being made? I would want to know what's going on. And I would want to make sure that my rep is going to keep me informed. That's the key thing that I am finding from this side of the desk that is being asked from managers. I would ask the same thing. Keep me informed. I don't want to be surprised. We notify our subscribers well in advance of changes that are taking place in our service so they understand what impact they may have.

We'd like the perception to continue that we're the only ballgame in town. There are obviously alternatives to Arbitron, or we would have every radio broadcaster signed up as a subscriber. We don't. The kind of options that people have is to take no report, which some do. Unfortunately, an awful lot of them try to steal it—an unfortunate fact of life for most research companies, and we're not the least of those that face that. You can take Birch, which some are doing. You have other companies like International Demographics and Scarborough—there's all sorts of those that come through. So there are lots of other opportunities. When I was selling and couldn't afford the Arbitron, I used RAB material.

The first thing that broadcasters must do is understand how a research company prices. What are my options? Are there discounts offered? What are the discounts generally, not only just for my station? There's nothing mysterious about what we do on pricing, yet there's a great fear of it.

Very simply, broadcasters should understand what their options are when it comes to pricing. I have a choice of a one, three, and five-year contract. "Well, what difference does that make to me? Are there discounts for long-term?" The answer to that is yes. "Well, what are the different discounts? Are there any price increases from year to year?" There are. "Well, what are they? How do they occur?" In other words, part of it is to understand how they're going to be priced. If they go through that process, I think they'll find out that they can take advantage of every discount we offer.

I really believe it's a matter of attitude. It's interesting, but the same attitude exists about the Radio Advertising Bureau. It's like RAB membership—well, I've got to have it. And yet that's not the proper attitude to make it work. The attitude, be it for RAB, NAB or Arbitron should be, "How am I going to get the most out of this tool?" When broadcasters have that kind of attitude, most of them find that there's lots and lots of ammunition to get out of it and use in their business.

What we generally do is have our sales staff go through the report and finds some little "gee whiz" things that they probably didn't even know about. And when they find out that that's indeed true, then they begin to say, "Well maybe it's got more in here than I thought it did."

The Arbitron book is like a gun; it's loaded with bullets—that's the data. Sending your sales staff out on the street, you provide each one of them with a gun, like a policeman. They know it's loaded. They hope they never have to use it, but you really want to make sure that they know how to use it in the event they have to. When broadcasters take that view of the Arbitron report, they then want to see how things are changing from one report to the next—see if they can determine the reasons why. If they take that kind of logical approach, they find it's very easy to deal with the subject, whether it's an up book, a down book, or consistent book, doesn't make any difference—it's still the book. Let's deal with what we've got. When they take that kind of approach, when they try to understand what's going on, we find that they can make very solid use of it because there's always a sales story for them.

Birch Viewpoints

Many of our station operators today have only lived in the world of Arbitron radio; they've never worked in television where there are two rating services. Many of them were not in a decision capacity when Arbitron was a little pup. So their whole mindset is geared toward Arbitron. Many of them are deathly afraid of cutting an umbilical cord by living without the Arbitron book. They feel that they'll fall into an abyss. They sense intuitively that something bad will happen. Consequently, the majority of broadcasters do not make a decision to drop Arbitron.

Television stations have found for many years that it's very valuable to have two rating services. If Nielsen says you have a six rating and Arbitron says you have a four rating, and if the agency is using Arbitron, the station needs to go in there and say "Hey look, Nielsen says we have a six," so they can possibly get themselves evaluated with a five or even that six as opposed to that four. The same should be true for radio.

In a world today that has become less dependent upon national agencies and more dependent on local ad revenue, it's become critical that a station describe itself beyond pure average quarter-hour estimates. Stations need to describe to an advertiser what the income of the audience is, what their occupation and product consumption habits are. These things have become absolutely critical to the gathering of local and regional dollars. It's become critical to Delta Airlines today. When Delta Airlines makes a buy, they look at Birch qualitative information—Birch quarterly information. Advertisers are going very quickly to the stage of wanting to look at radio differently. All they have to do is look at a market like Los Angeles where just about every radio station has a two share. An advertiser's plight is to say, "What's the difference between any of them?" They have to look beyond the quarter-hour estimates.

Most of our broadcast clients are not schooled in the technical aspects of the research business. Arbitron may be a lot of things to a lot of people, but they're not dishonest when it comes to performing their measurement. They perform what they say they're going to perform. And they go out and measure a marketplace with a diary and then they produce those results—regardless of who subscribes or who does not subscribe. But many broadcasters do not believe that. They believe that the ratings are skewed to favor subscribers.

We all have a need to know what we're buying. If I advertise, I want to know what the station's presenting to me. The easiest way that most stations default is by saying, "I'm in this demographic." The creative broadcasters, in contrast, describe their stations in different terms. "Our audience is mid-income, it reflects the marketplace; it's generally blue collar and it reflects the marketplace; it has a tendency to buy a lot of automobiles." These people have been extremely successful because they have walked away from the easy approach to a sales problem.

Radio Rating Services: Negotiating Exercise

The negotiation exercises below will allow you to focus on your own experiences. Even if you are new to these negotiations, the exercises will allow you to plan better for your forthcoming negotiations.

This exercise is designed for you to focus on common thorny issues that frequently arise in the course of negotiating with radio ratings services. It is useful to review these concerns before a negotiation in this area in order to anticipate what your response would be if these situations arise. Review these questions with your staff to reassess your policies, as warranted.

1. Arbitron comes in with a new five-year contract for you to sign, but at a substantially higher rate. How do you respond?

2. Birch wants to make a presentation soon, despite the fact that all of your competition in the market use Arbitron. How receptive are you to be hearing from Birch?

3. Will your decision to renew with Arbitron be influenced if some sweeteners are added to the deal, such as lower prices for the summer and winter books? If so, which ones?

4. What information on methodological improvements will you insist upon during the negotiation (e.g., data on diary non-responses)?

5. What if Arbitron makes its presentation, and ends with "an offer you can't refuse" provided you sign today? Will you?

6. How will you utilize your sales force to develop information that indicates Arbitron is nice to have but not essential?

7. Are you willing to walk away from Arbitron on the basis of price alone?

8. What in-house research capabilities can be bolstered to offset the loss of Arbitron?

9. What if Arbitron backs down and is willing to lower its price, but for a one year term instead?

10. What happens if your negotiation with Arbitron ends without a contract and you sign with Birch for much less money? Six months later, Arbitron comes back to make another presentation to sign you up next year at the same price you had been paying. Are you receptive to this pitch, or are you skeptical based on your recent unsuccessful negotiation experience?

Radio Ratings Services: Strategic and Tactical Negotiating Considerations

Now that you given some thought to these negotiations and heard from others involved, you can best evaluate some recommendations. In the following pages, we offer some concluding recommendations. Consider these when planning your next negotiation with any of the rating service firms, and build upon them with some of your own.

History of Ratings Negotiations

In its October 20, 1986 issue, *Radio News* reported as one of its major stories the ongoing renewal negotiations between Bonneville Broadcasting and Arbitron. The coverage provided a rare public glimpse over what goes on behind the scenes, and it bears highlighting here.

The first meeting between the parties took place in August 1986. The issue on the agenda was the renewal of Bonneville's contract with Arbitron for a five-year term. No agreement was reached. A second meeting was held in early October, this time with those on both sides who had full negotiating authority. According to *Radio News*, Bonneville's position to Arbitron was "Too expensive. Drop your rate or we (Bonneville) will drop you."

Bonneville thus became one of the first major radio broadcast groups (RKO was another) to challenge Arbitron strictly on rates. Increasingly, individual broadcasters and the NAB itself are becoming more vocal about counteracting Arbitron's leverage as a provider of radio ratings services. The complacent days of merely signing on the dotted line and writing a check appear to be over.

NAB's Radio Audience Measurement Task Force

The NAB Radio Board unanimously approved the establishment of the Radio Audience Measurement Task Force (RAMTF) in January 1985. This Task Force was originally proposed by the NAB's Medium Market Radio Committee, which had expressed frustration with radio ratings accuracy, runaway spiral costs and the quality of audience measurement. RAMTF was charged with examining whether there were opportunities for alternative means of measuring radio listening. It sought requests for proposals from the entire research industry and received 22 responses. After all respondents were interviewed, three were selected to receive $5,000 grants from the NAB to further develop their proposals. Of this group, two accepted RAMTF's request to conduct a field test of their systems in Gainesville, Florida. These two firms, Birch Radio of Coral Springs, Florida, and McNair-Anderson of North Sydney, Australia, also made presentations of their ratings methodology, along with Arbitron, at the NAB's 1987 convention in Dallas.

During this period, RAMTF became aware that some of the 22 bidding firms had apprehensions about entering the radio ratings business. These apprehensions were based on uncertainty about what barriers to entering this market exist and what economic opportunities there are. With NAB board approval, RAMTF authorized the hiring of an outside firm to study the economic and legal aspects of the radio audience ratings marketplace as it exists today. The full report subsequently was forwarded to the NAB Executive Committee.

The report's highlights include these findings:

- Arbitron represents a monopoly in this market. By virtue of its "monopoly" status, Arbitron has the power to raise rates and set standards. Its position as a "classic" monopolist, however, is not by itself illegal. The law restrains monopolies only when monopolists abuse that status.

- Arbitron's use of five-year contracts does not appear to represent an illegal "barrier to entry" since there are escape clauses being negotiated. Additionally, Birch finds no harm caused by this practice, and is itself offering comparable contracts with cancellation clauses.

- If there is a barrier to entry, it is in the reluctance of advertising agencies to accept a new radio ratings service. Much of this reluctance stems from agencies' computer software, which primarily accesses Arbitron information.

- There is both confusion and lack of knowledge among broadcasters relating to the methods by which Arbitron and Birch establish their rates. Contrary to the perception of some broadcasters, Arbitron no longer uses the rate card system for pricing its services. The study found that pricing does not appear to be cost-based, but rather is based primarily on TSA cumes and market size. Arbitron maintained, however, that pricing is based on TSA cumes, not market size. Birch uses a cost-plus-profit pricing method.

- Where Birch is in a market, Arbitron prices are lower, which seems to confirm that competition does, in fact, lead to lower prices. Differences in cost to stations between the two services range three to four times higher for Arbitron than for Birch.

Other Broadcasters' Tactics

RAMTF's activities have contributed to a gradual shift in Arbitron's negotiating behavior. So have events in the field. What strategies are radio managers using to negotiate with Arbitron? Some comments derived during the confidential interviews that were conducted for this book present ideas worth noting.

1. Utilize buying power. Volume buying often can give you greater leverage in obtaining a better deal. If you are part of a station group, try to coordinate negotiations with ratings services so that you can take advantage of any available volume discounts.

> "Arbitron is quite inflexible in their main contract. I think the bottom line of Arbitron is that if you know where your position is, sometimes things can be changed. They appear to be inflexible, but if you have group clout or if you want some of the additional features or you have a circumstance that indicates that you're in the driver's seat, there's some room for negotiation. They have usually been willing to talk about things."

2. Argue that all users should bear a fair share of costs. Radio ratings services benefit a number of parties besides broadcasters. As the following comments of a radio manager reveal, this point needs to be articulated more forcefully throughout the media community and to the ratings services themselves during negotiations.

> "The next time you negotiate with Arbitron, I think you have to insist on a dramatically reduced rate for your research information. I think it's high time the advertiser started paying a larger share of the local market ratings data that's being produced. It's time the load is put onto the advertiser. We're the most powerful, the most effective, the most intrusive medium that's ever been invented or ever will be invented. We don't have to justify our numbers. We don't have to justify that our medium works. We know it works better than any other. It's the best medium for a message. But the day has got to stop where we're paying 90 percent of those costs. More of that cost has to be assumed by the advertiser and by your competitors such as cable systems."

3. Cancel service and pursue other alternatives. The importance of subscribing to a radio rating service should be re-evaluated prior to entering a renewal negotiation. Remember, there are costs of not renewing—the use of the Continuous Service Discount, post publication surcharge and increased rates. Yet, perhaps the possibility of canceling and pursuing other alternatives is more realistic than you originally thought.

> "I think the best leverage a broadcaster has in negotiating with the ratings companies, specifically Arbitron, is to cancel. Broadcasters who have had the intestinal fortitude to drop Arbitron—to say, 'I'm dropping it'—have negotiated with Arbitron significantly lower rates than they were offered. I'm defining cancelling as meaning not signing the contract on a deadline, doing without it for a period of months, maybe a year. Any station that signs a contract by Arbitron's deadline did not get the best rate. They have failed in that negotiation."

Final Recommendations

Of all the topics covered in this book, negotiating with Arbitron presents the greatest number of practical concerns. Arbitron appears to have all the leverage. Cumulatively, the process of transforming the purchase of Arbitron services from a routine sales transaction to one where both parties recognize a greater sense of give-and-take will, at best, be a gradual one. This give-and-take will occur if broadcasters begin to be more active in these negotiations. A few final points broadcasters should consider when planning for negotiations with the radio ratings companies are:

- The past year has been critical because events indicate that the radio industry is interested in exploring options that can be implemented outside the negotiating process. The availability of potential alternatives such as Birch or doing without a ratings service should instill more confidence among radio broadcasters who enter a negotiation with Arbitron. If stations choose to walk away, they can do so with such options in mind. Radio managers would be well advised to gather as much information as possible about these options before meeting with Arbitron.

- Broadcasters should also encourage competition by being receptive to presentations by Birch and others if available in their markets. And they should listen long and hard to their advertising salespeople to gain a better sense of just how useful Arbitron is in the ad sales process. Some broadcasters may be pleasantly surprised to find that advertisers and their agencies are willing to look beyond ratings when making a radio buy. This knowledge is powerful information to have prior to a negotiation in order to bolster your argument for lower rates due to decreased value. The views of advertisers represent objective criteria that can be used in your favor. You should make every effort to obtain documentation to support this argument, such as solicited letters from key accounts or the results of commissioned market research that surveys the attitudes of the advertising community.

- Radio managers also need to raise their aspiration levels when negotiating with Arbitron. Information derived from Chester L. Karrass' experimental research, which is summarized in his book *The Negotiation Game* (T. W. Carrol, 1970), indicates that persons with higher aspiration levels won higher awards (the goal of the experiment) in negotiations. In other words, those who started out wanting more ended by getting more.

Many of the interviews with radio managers revealed a sense of quiet resignation, if not outright defeat, regarding their ability to negotiate with Arbitron on the basis of price. The comments of one manager represent the views of many. "I think the alcoholic's prayer of 'God give me the courage to change the things I can, the patience for things I can't and the wisdom to know the difference' is the driving force in any negotiation with Arbitron," he said. Low aspiration levels such as this are likely to become self-fulfilling prophecies if such attitudes are brought to the negotiation table. Moreover, keep in mind that the RAMTF's commissioned economic and legal analysis concluded that broadcasters who negotiate their rates received concessions not received by those who do not.

"If I were negotiating with Arbitron," an industry insider told me, "I would say, 'Here's the rate I'm willing to pay' and I would predicate that on what I felt was fair. And I would tell them that I want every service that Arbitron gives with that rate. I wouldn't be ridiculous, but I'd be fair, and then I would tell them, 'You can accept it or not, otherwise I'll use Birch exclusively.' Then I would be prepared to cancel my contract, knowing that Arbitron representative would be back in my office with another offer. Every station or operator that has done that has accomplished a great deal." Perhaps that's the best advice that can be offered on negotiating rates with Arbitron for the foreseeable future.

- Broadcasters also should keep in mind that Arbitron is a service company, and that negotiations may involve disucssions about what level of service is being offered given Arbitron's high price tag. Beyond price, broadcast managers should adopt an aggressive attitude in seeking additional books or special services. While Arbitron states it will not provide free books, it does offer discounts on additional reports. Demands for more personalized service also appear to be reasonable under the circumstances.

- Finally, despite its imposing nature, the Arbitron contract should not be viewed as a document that cannot be modified through negotiation. It is common knowledge that special deals have been negotiated by Arbitron in recent years, and broadcasters should assume that contract changes can be made. Two examples come to mind. First, some managers have been able to negotiate favorable exit terms, allowing them to cancel a contract at the end of any year during a five-year term without penalty. Arbitron has in place, however, a short rate policy where upon cancellation of a long term contact leads to a higher rate charged for the years during which services were provided. Others have sought to have a "most favored nation" clause inserted in their contracts. Such a clause allows them to receive comparable special treatment if Arbitron offers it to a competitor in the same market. Expect resistance on both fronts, but don't be afraid to press Arbitron on details that may be advantageous to you.

Conclusion

Negotiating with radio ratings service companies present an interesting situation because there are not many firms with which to negotiate. Yet, with careful planning any radio station can be (and may have been) successful in those negotiations.

Television Programming Syndication: An Overview

In terms of frequency, the two negotiations already discussed are the polar cases. Advertising negotiations occur every day while radio ratings service negotiations occur, at most, every year. The next set of negotiations occur more often than radio ratings services, but not every day as with advertising sales. Yet, planning and evaluating for television programming negotiations, in part, occur every day. Those deals involve considerable amounts of money and requires significant amounts of time. Negotiating skills in this process can improve a television station's bottom line in a big way.

The Syndication Process

Syndication refers to the licensing of programs for exhibition to individual television stations. Syndicated entertainment program offerings comprise three general categories: first-run, off-network, and movies. Local stations acquire the rights to broadcast syndicated programs by executing agreements with program producers or their agents. In most cases, the station pays a license fee for the exhibition rights and recoups its investment by selling commercial spots within the program. With barter syndication, the station acquires a program with certain commercial announcements already inserted; the remaining commercial availability is allocated for the station's use.

There are three categories of producers who supply syndicated programming. Off-network producers make available repeat exhibitions of prime-time series. Typically, it is the revenues from syndication that make prime-time production a profitable undertaking. Without this additional source of revenue for a successful series, networks would have to pay substantially higher license fees for the initial exhibition rights in order to maintain the type and quality of programs on their schedules.

First-run producers produce programs specifically for syndication. The producers of network daytime game shows are among the most important contributors to the first-run syndication market. Finally, foreign producers have become an important source of syndicated programming in recent years.

Syndicators have the responsibility for contacting and negotiating with individual stations for the exhibition rights to programs. Usually, a syndicator obtains the right to distribute a program from the program producer who owns it. In exchange for its effort to distribute the program to stations, the syndicator receives a specified percentage of the amount paid by the station for the exhibition rights. Some syndicators produce as well as distribute programs, thus increasing their revenue potential.

An individual station's demand for syndicated programs depends in large measure on whether or not it is affiliated with a network. A network-affiliated station is compensated by the network for clearing its programs, and is thus less reliant on purchasing outside product. Independent stations, in contrast, must purchase virtually all of their programs in the syndication marketplace.

First-run series are perceived by some within the industry as having less desirability than off-network series and feature films in terms of syndication desirability. To them, off-network series and feature films have a proven track record and are generally of higher cost than first-run syndicated programming. Revenues from off-network series must be sufficient to cover only distribution costs and residual fees. First-run programs, however, must meet similar distribution costs plus full production costs.

Off-Network Programs

Local stations sometimes must wait for the expiration of the exclusivity protection given the network in its contract with the program producer before it can exhibit repeats of network program series. A producer's negotiations with a syndicator, however, often occur early in the program production process, sometimes even during the program's development stage. Network exclusivity does not prohibit the foreign exhibition of the series simultaneous with its first-run on a U.S. network, which presents the possibility of immediately returning revenues to the producer to supplement the network license fees.

There are four major issues in negotiations between a producer of a network series and a syndicator. These are: (1) the basic arrangement for dividing revenues; (2) the duration of the syndicator's distribution rights; (3) the territory in which the program may be sold; and (4) monetary advances. The most lucrative syndication market, by far, is the domestic market. It is in the mutual interest of both syndicators and producers that the programs enjoy the widest possible domestic distribution at the highest license fees.

There are certain factors that may affect the syndication success of an off-network series. The most important characteristic common to all off-network syndicated programs is a successful run in network prime time in order to provide enough episodes to be salable in domestic syndication. Prime-time popularity also helps measure a series' chances of success in syndication.

First-Run Programs

In first-run syndication, producers, syndicators, and stations share the risk of the enterprise succeeding outside the established network system. The program producer approaches one or more syndicators with a concept for a program. The commitment of the syndicator is often conditioned on its ability to obtain promises from stations to purchase the program. The type of program produced for first-run syndication usually is significantly less expensive than the typical network prime-time series. Syndicated programs usually will not be purchased by affiliated stations for prime-time exhibition because they can obtain network offerings during that time period. They usually show syndicated programs during non-prime-time hours that do not generate the same advertising revenues as prime time. Unaffiliated commercial stations do not provide the same total market coverage and therefore, provide a smaller base for apportioning program costs. Thus, the markets available for syndicated programs typically will not support expensive first-run programming, although there are some notable exceptions. Moreover, distributing individual programs to stations substantially increases the operating costs above those for simultaneous interconnection.

In the prime time access time period, situation comedies and dramatic series have proven far typically less successful than game shows and, to a lesser extent, variety programs. Producers generally share the same incentives as the stations. They both want to develop a program that is likely to appeal to the access period audience but is sufficiently inexpensive so that the production costs can be recovered from sales to relatively few stations.

Barter Programs

Some syndicated programs are distributed to stations by bartering the exhibition license in exchange for advertising time on the stations. True barter typically involves the distribution of a program that already contains a certain number of commercial announcements as well as a certain number of unfilled commercial spots. In contrast, with time banking barter, the program does not contain any commercial inserts. Instead, the station agrees to place the advertiser's commercials at specified times in other programs.

The joining of forces by Paramount TV, Coca-Cola Telecommunications and Orbis Communications to sell all of their barter time under one umbrella (International Advertising Sales) may be the harbinger of a major new trend toward consolidation. Advertising agency buyers of barter syndication find such consolidation to be advantageous since larger operations can offer the advertiser the equivalent of a full schedule, with series in all the dayparts.

At the 1987 NATPE convention, syndicators unveiled an unprecedented number of new barter shows. These are perceived by some syndicators as a safety valve in the weakening market for cash shows. Many stations that cannot pay for a show might be willing to take the program for "free" via barter. The strongest station in a market typically disdains barter because the show takes commercial time that could be sold locally. The big surge in barter programming could have a devastating effect on barter commercial pricing, since 100 new barter shows represent 20,000 30-second units. With this type of glut, barter advertisers could face a buyer's market characterized by a significant drop in barter rates.

Financial Considerations

Almost all stations—even network affiliates for whom the network is a major source of programming—bid for programs in the syndication market. When all stations enter the bidding wars for syndicated programs, the license fees paid for program exhibition rights inevitably increase, reducing some of the profits for broadcasters. Competition among stations to obtain programs allows the program supplier to extract higher fees for any given program or series in the larger markets. There is nothing in the law or in the economics of the syndication market to prevent program distributors from discriminating in price based on market size, and the natural tendency of stations to compete in the market for programs strengthens this practice.

Syndicated program prices are the outcome of a bargaining process between syndicators and stations. In markets where there are a small number of stations and small potential audiences, prices are likely to be low, close to the marginal costs of distributing the programs. In the larger markets, syndicators can capture more of the broadcast revenue due to increased demand and bidding by stations.

A large syndicator typically has 400-500 client stations. One syndicator said that there are about 40 or 50 stations on its list that are 90-180 days behind their payments on programming buys. If a station were to completely shut down, the syndicator would receive nothing. In Chapter 11 bankruptcy, stations can restructure their business while protecting it from creditors. In that case, a syndicator is forced to continue to supply programming even though the station is behind in payments.

If a station has difficulty making the payments, it may ask for a reduction in the program's price, a lengthening of the payment terms, or permission to completely drop some of the shows that it previously contracted to run. Syndicators often renegotiate under these circumstances.

The rise in syndicated programming costs has been largely attributable to demand for product from independent stations. That trend is slowing down. With fewer independent stations starting up, and others seeking to keep costs in line, the demand for syndicated programming has leveled off during the past two years. As one broadcaster commented, "Austerity has begun to play a greater role in program bargaining than I have seen in well over a decade."

Between 1971 and 1983 advertising revenues climbed annually an average of 14 percent, according to the estimates of Robert Coen of McCann-Erikson, New York. Furthermore, more independent television stations came on the air; the number of independents doubled between 1980 and 1985, and they were clamoring for off-network programs. In short, syndication demand was high and program supply was limited. By 1983, union wages and Hollywood's production budgets were still growing at double-digit rates, but advertising revenue growth dropped to single digits.

Traditionally, Hollywood had been content with fees from the networks on hour and half-hour series that nearly covered production costs because there were such hefty profits in syndicating the reruns. Under recently changed economic conditions, the networks began refusing to come close to covering production costs.

At the same time, stations have fewer dollars to spend on programming because of a tougher spot advertising marketplace nationally and sluggish local sales in some markets. Deals for most shows are written on a tiered basis, with license fees varying depending upon the time periods they ultimately occupy.

For example, in a higher HUT-level time period such as prime-time access, a license fee would be higher than for early fringe or daytime.

Block booking has recently become more significant in television syndication. This has come about because of the fierce battle among syndicators for the lucrative 4-8 p.m. time periods. Program suppliers want to lock up these time periods by combining a successful program with other programming. Thus, if they have one big hit, they seek to leverage other, less attractive programs with it.

There is a shortage of both available time periods and programs that work. A station thus may take less desirable shows in order to get the program that it wants. This practice, known as block booking, raises antitrust law concerns when initiated by syndicators. Block booking is the conditioning or tying of the sale of one product to another. Not every package sale is necessarily illegal. For example, buyers may request a package for a reduced rate. In order to create a block booking violation of law, in contrast, there must be both a minimum of two products and sufficient economic power with the desirable one to force the taking of the one that the buyer does not want.

Conclusion

The balance of power in the syndicated marketplace tends to shift back and forth between buyer and seller every few years. Most recently, buyers appear to be gaining the upper hand. This year, according to *Variety*, "dozens of first-run syndicated pilots that roared into January's NATPE convention with high hopes of getting a launch are now dead." The reason: "one of the most harshly competitive selling seasons ever."

Sellers are offering too many programs to fill too few available time periods. That puts stations in the driver's seat, at least as far as new product is concerned. On the other hand, it may weaken their negotiating position regarding proven hits, which can capitalize on an otherwise soft market by increasing their price and scheduling demands.

The equilibrium between buyer and seller is bound to become more balanced again over time. Broadcasters would be well advised not to accept their current strong position in the program syndication market as a given. Driving a hard bargain now may pay off in the short-term, but it could also damage long-term relations with the syndicators.

Television Programming Syndication: The Viewpoints of Broadcast Managers

Faced with the new marketplace and experiences from the most recent years, how do broadcasters see the buying and selling of programming? What goes into the planning for programming? How do broadcasters evaluate their station's ability to buy certain programming? Partial answers to these questions are in the quotes of broadcasters below.

I think syndicators have a very difficult job. I think the business that they are in is a difficult one. And they're very aggressive. Some of them lie and some of them do some shady dealings. But overall, I work very hard trying to maintain a really good relationship with syndicators because they're the lifeblood of my business as an independent station. And they're also the lifeblood, in many cases, for affiliates. I think if you treat a syndicator fairly and you respect the syndicator for the tough job he has, I think he's going to give you a break down the line somewhere in the negotiation.

You should know more about the market than they do. We don't, usually. They have a better handle, but we should. We ought to know what possibilities he has to move the product in the market, play our best card, and if we don't win, go on to Plan B, because there's always something coming down the pike.

I've been in the business a long time and I've heard every year from syndicators that there's no more property coming down the line, there's not going to be anything. And every year it's always coming down. There's a ton of something being developed.

Number one, always take their call and when they come to town, try to be the first one to see them. I would spend time with them just as if they are your biggest department store account or your biggest grocery chain account. Because if you can build that relationship, then there are little things they could do to help you down the road.

We have to live with people on that side of the desk forever. And they have to live with us forever. There are a couple that I just won't see, no matter what they're selling, because they have been dishonest, unfair. But I have nothing against somebody coming into this market and trying to maximize his product. That's his job.

Know your market. Know your competition. Know your schedule and know what the positioning of your station in the marketplace is or what you plan on it being. When a syndicator comes in, treat him as though you were sitting on the other side of the desk. You don't play games and you don't try to snow him and you don't try to come off very hard. He's out to make a buck and you're out to make a buck and if you can build a certain empathy and a certain friendship and you accept his professionalism, then he will accept your professionalism. In the trading of knowledge, the two of you will reach a point where you establish an ongoing relationship that can aid both sides.

You try and predict the attitude of your competition. We keep accurate records of what they bought. Syndicators are such sharp, sharp salespeople because they know every bit of product I have. They know my competition. They know their competition. And when they come into a marketplace they are so strong, so well armed.

You'd better know your market very well and you'd better have a good fix on the operating philosophy of your competitors. You have to know where the opportunities lie and you've got to do a lot of anticipating on what competitors might do because that will help you in keeping your cost in line when negotiating with syndicators.

To a large extent you've got to have a good feel for what your competitors might have, how a particular program might fit in with your competitor's schedule. If you don't see that there's much of a market or opportunity for the syndicator to place that show on another station at a time period that might be advantageous to him, then you have a very strong negotiating posture. They need you almost as much as you need them, and maybe sometimes more.

You've got to take into account where the syndicator can go. If the syndicator's got another home to go to on the market, you're going to have to be a lot more flexible than you are if the syndicator has no other place to go.

We do not plan. We do not, in my judgment, do anything with a great degree of sophistication. We should be looking at the number of units we have for sale in a time period, we should be looking at the potential audience value of the program, the cost per point we can get, the gross revenue. We should determine how much of that we want to give to the syndicator. We shouldn't be cutting deals in which by the time we get through, we discover we've given all the profits to the syndicator.

Television Programming Syndication: The Viewpoints of Syndicators

Syndicators are in a very risky business. Sometimes they have broadcasters beating down their door, other times they have great difficulty selling their product. How do they approach the negotiating table? What do they look for in the other side? How do they try and sell their different products? The thoughts of various syndicators on these and other issues are presented below.

Broadcasters make their decisions on syndicated buys based on the type of programming that they're going to have on their television station. They want to get the best shows possible and program them so that the flow and the programs work together.

A good broadcast negotiator basically is one who conducts the negotiation in a rational manner, who tries to maintain a relationship.

Several factors enter into a negotiation aside from money. There's the time period, the strength of the station, the station's ability to promote. These factors are key ones.

Good broadcast negotiators reflect a preparedness about the performance of their station relative to my program and my program relative to their station's success, or lack of it. Their competitive stance, timing, and the place and time when bidding is done also come to mind. These negotiators are in tune with the state of my program, my company, my costs, my success inside and outside the market. They are knowledgeable enough to understand where I'm going, maybe even head me off at the pass. They place themselves in a position of understanding what it is they want at the end; they are goal-oriented.

Broadcasters should really get to know our business, too. If they got to know our business a little bit more and understood the syndication end of it, it certainly would help. For example, I hear this a lot.

"I only promised my board or my group no more than a 20 percent increase." My response to that is, "Well, why did you do that? Let's be realistic. Let's say we sold you the show for $1000 a day last year. That's fair price when you're buying a new product or a product that maybe wasn't where it was yet, and you did very well. The cost per point is maybe $100, you're doing 10 rating points, that's $1000 a spot. Net it down and you're getting $800 a spot or something like that. Don't you think that you should pay for the results? So therefore, why shouldn't the price be—and I'm just picking numbers—$3000 this year? What is the return that you expect from your investment in syndicated property? What do you think is a fair deal?" Let's look at it from the syndicators' point of view. In other words, broadcasters often focus on the wrong benchmark.

If a show is doing extremely well, we hope that we deserve a price increase. We'll then explain it to the television station: our research based on what it's done and what we project it will do. We will show the station a revenue analysis. We will discuss our asking price with them. We will listen to the station, try to negotiate a fair price. The salesman's responsibility is to know what's going on in the marketplace. Any good salesman must always know what's going on in the marketplace in a competitive situation, and know what will happen if for some reason we cannot make a deal with the incumbent.

As a company, we adhere to the "stay with me" affiliation process. We have found this to be as successful as pushing a broadcaster against the wall with an ability to either leverage or threaten. Unfortunately, threats are used on both sides of the negotiation table. They are historic to local broadcasting. The fear in local broadcasting is that if I don't move now, the guy down the street will. That ever present fear is always on the table. In fact, a commonly heard line in a negotiation between a syndicator and a buyer in a renewal process is from the buyer, "I know that nobody else in town wants you," and on the other side, from the syndicator who will say, "If we can't do business, there's a guy across the street who's waiting for me." The guns are usually loaded prematurely because most programs are not successful enough to carry the negotiation on their own weight.

I'm a believer in staying with your customer because they have a track on you, they have a promotion record on you, they can build on their past.

As an independent, I would be tempted to plan further ahead in projecting my programming for two or three years at a time, knowing the buying patterns of what I'm going to face and having a general idea of how the networks would fare against me. And then I'd be much more tempted to play with the structure than most of the industry does today. I would play with the clock, I would play with moving genres away from competitive genres of the same breed.

There has been a myth about barter syndication for all of barter's history. Recently that's been modified considerably because of the extent that most broadcasters are now involved in some kind of barter. There is an ongoing myth of syndicators being only concerned with what they can take out and not putting anything back. That myth of the typical syndicator, if you will, is one that I have attempted to destroy personally in my company.

We suffer generically in the first-run and in the barter business in terms of promotion because if we cost less, sometimes we get promoted less. The mentality of too many station managers is to put your money where you spend your money. Barter has no cost design to it in many instances, or it has a lower cost. Therefore, we suffer in the promotion game because we don't cost enough—it's a very strange, very strange circumstance.

First-run product is much more of a theoretical sell, much more a conceptual sell. An off-network product has performed to a level and it is then relegated to a performance on a station based on its experience with that product type historically. First-run is a breed that has limited experience in terms of a genre, if it is in fact original. And first-run is diverse, more varied. It is a much more difficult sell because of its lack of a network track record.

The pioneer spirit aligns to investing in first-run programming, knowing that by getting into an initial position, broadcasters can generally buy in cheaper and for the long run make a better deal for themselves. But it takes a great deal of courage to turn around to management and say I'm taking a higher risk with a new genre.

If you can receive a first-run program idea and genre as generic to your schedule, that's step one. We then can deal with cost and application against what you are facing. But you must like the concept and idea, see it in a counterprogram position. Generally, you'll wind up paying less for the initial first-run program. Your cost might become equivalent to other categories as it succeeds.

Cultivate the syndicators. Get to know them, their problems. Tell them what your problems are, stay in touch with them, have an open communication with them at all times and always see every syndicator. You never know when the next mega-hit is going to walk in.

Honesty in the long term will always pay off, as far as we're concerned. When I deal with an individual and trust that individual, I know that the negotiation is going to proceed with a lot less hassle.

Television Programming Syndication: Negotiating Exercise

Many of the previous quotes should have sound familiar. Either you have felt these words or have heard them from other broadcasters and syndicators. In order to more fully focus in on your approach to syndication negotiations, the following exercise is presented.

This exercise is designed for you to focus on common thorny issues that frequently arise in the course of negotiating the acquisition of first-run, off-network and barter syndicated television programming. It is useful to review these concerns before a negotiation in this area in order to anticipate what your responses would be if these situations arise. Discuss these issues with your program staff to elicit their opinions.

1. A syndicator presents to you an attractive series available next season, but you feel the price is too high given your overall programming budget. How do you respond?

2. The syndicator emphasizes this is an off-network series with a great network track record behind it. How do you respond?

3. The off-network series has been in syndication for two years, and during this time has developed a track record in comparable markets to yours. Does this information change your response? If so, how?

4. What if the series is first-run with no prior track record?

5. What if the first-run series is being offered on a barter basis?

6. What if the syndicator is offering an attractive program as well as several others that are less attractive but capable of fitting into your schedule. Are you willing to take one of these in order to improve your changes of striking a good deal for the program you really want?

7. What do you do if you have information that a competitor in the market will buy the series if your negotiation does not end with a buy?

8. What do you do if you suspect that the syndicator is using you to bid up the price so that he can bring it to a competitor for a final bid to top yours?

9. How is your negotiating leverage affected by your long-standing relationship with the syndicator?

10. What if you take a package for which both sides have optimistic but modest expectations? With proper scheduling and promotion, the series becomes a big winner both nationally and within your market. The syndicator returns the following year with a new, long-term deal. How does your renegotiating strategy differ from your original negotiating strategy? Is it affected by learning that your competition is anxious to buy the rights instead in order to boost its sagging ratings in a key time period?

Television Programming Syndication: Strategic and Tactical Negotiating Considerations

The previous exercise should have led to some reflection on the syndication negotiation process. Coupled with the opinions of the two sides in the prior sections, you should have a better understanding of this actual situation. With all that in mind, we offer a few recommendations. Hopefully they will only be the seeds for your own future actions in these negotiations.

The television programming syndication marketplace is like a pendulum. It swings back and forth every few years between being a seller's market and a buyer's market. Accordingly, the first strategic consideration is not to become too disappointed or enthralled by what the market looks like at any particular point in time. You will be buying syndicated product year in and year out. As a result, it's best to keep your eye on both the long-term and the short-run.

Specific Recommendations

In today's buyer's market, there may be a tendency among some managers to become cocky, perhaps even to extract a measure of revenge for all the times that syndicators exercised the upper hand. Avoid any such temptations. The best course to follow, regardless of who the market favors, involves building relationships within the syndication community; understanding your station's needs over time; and staying on top of—and hopefully ahead of—what your competitors are buying. Let's cover these fundamentals by reviewing advice offered about them by television managers who were interviewed for this book:

1. Building relationships. The human dimension of negotiations always should be kept in mind. You are likely to have ongoing contact with the other side in future transactions. Because of this, you must focus on your long-term relationship as well as the outcome of the immediate negotiation.

"I have developed over the years superb vendor relationships. One of the things I find very useful is to treat them like human beings. Because when they have something that you really need, they are going to give whatever edge they can to people who have been nice to them. You tend to forget that these are dads and mothers just like you, with children and all the same realities that you have. I find if you nourish them with a little respect, that cumulatively over the course of the years you may have some dividends. We go out to lunch with them. Every once in a while we go out to dinner with them. You know, there's an old saying, 'If you don't see Mama Monday through Friday, you might not see Mama on Saturday night.' It applies here, for sure."

2. Understanding your station's needs over time. A long-term view is equally important when evaluating what your station's goals are. The better you can project future needs, the better your ability will be to negotiate a current deal that you won't regret later on.

"We've set up a computerized formula in which we are determining the profitability of a program based on what it costs. There's a whole formula we have where we determine the cost of the program. We find out what rate our sales manager could get for us; normally, we're dealing with three or four years from now."

3. Keeping track of the competition. It is not necessary to love your neighbor, but it certainly helps if you know what your competitors down the road are doing. Competitive intelligence allows you to position your station for a more favorable outcome during a negotiation for syndicated programming.

"I feel it's extremely important that I know what the competitive situation in the market has been, is now and is most likely to be. For instance, what commitments do the other stations have? What product do they have on the shelf? What is their standard operating procedure? Everyone leaves certain tracks."

Other Considerations

Now that you have a sense of the basics, here are some special considerations to add to the picture.

- First, consider what building a relationship really means. Although the social aspects may be pleasant, you build a relationship with the other side in order to get as good a feel as possible for how his/her business operates. This allows you to develop strategies and tactics that can put money in the syndicator's pocketbook as well as yours.

  Building a relationship is not an abstract process; you must seek to satisfy the individual needs of their side as well as the company needs they represent. Here's a true story told by a television manager that makes this point in far more graphic terms, and with very graphic results:

  > "The psychological advantage we like to gain is to anticipate what he might think. And if we know that he might not be a prospect for the piece of programming that we are looking at, we are in a tremendously advantageous position. It's Friday afternoon. The syndicator's representative has had a nice lunch; maybe he's had a cold Coors beer. Now he's coming back to the office, right, and he's got to tell someone how the hell has the week been? What has he sold? There is a sales manager somewhere who wants to know what happened this week. By waiting till Friday afternoon—I've got litany after litany of deals that I cut—if a guy's had a rough week and there's nothing on the sales order book, you're in a position to have him suddenly be a part of your negotiating team because he wants to cut a deal. He doesn't want to go with a whitewash for the week. Field syndicators have to report to sales managers on Friday afternoons. That fact alone has saved us thousands of dollars over the years."

- The competitive nature of the syndication marketplace can and should always be used to your advantage. You should enter the negotiation with a clear idea of what product you would buy— and under what terms—if your negotiation with a particular syndicator breaks down. In strategic terms, be aware of your options and don't be afraid to reveal them during a negotiation if they are strong. The stronger they are, the more assertively you will be able to negotiate. As one manager noted, "I think you have to let the syndicator know that there are other vehicles available that you'd be interested in. I think you have to constantly try to create the feeling that you have other options, other ways to fill your schedule. If I can show the syndicator that I have other vehicles that are just as powerful to me, I think it gives me flexibility in negotiation."

- Syndicated programming, even programming with great performance on a network in previous years, always must establish its own track record as a syndicated property, and in various time periods. Broadcast managers can take advantage of this reality both when a show is first offered for syndication and when it is seeking to re-establish its reputation in a new time slot (e.g., from early fringe to prime-time access). In effect, by taking a chance on programming with a lesser track record in either sense, you can negotiate better terms. The syndicator benefits by being able to charge higher rates to others once the show proves to be a hit, and thus should be receptive to your proposal. Here's one broadcast manager explaining how this strategy worked in practice:

  > "If *Jeopardy* happened to be running on a competing station at 4 o'clock, doing very well around the country, I look at that show to go in at 7 o'clock on our station. That move can be attractive for the syndicator. If I hold a possibility of a 7 o'clock time period out to them, I might get that show with far less in terms of the cash that I might pay simply because it's important to them to get on at 7 o'clock and establish a track record there."

  Remember what I said about the pendulum swinging back and forth? Take heed of the cautionary footnote that this same broadcast manager commented on: "After a show has done significantly well in establishing a track record, of course, the challenge for me will be to keep that show at an affordable price. Most of the negotiating leverage goes over to the syndicator at that point," the manager said with both a sigh and a chuckle.

- The importance of doing your homework well in advance of the negotiation is a central theme of this book. Given the complexity of the formulas you will be developing to project future revenue needs (which must account for inflation and unforeseen events, among other factors), let me reemphasize here the risk you run by not understanding your numbers or how they were derived. Without such information readily at hand, you may find yourself nodding in agreement as the syndicator presents his/her own version of a formula that seems reasonable to all.

But is it? According to one interviewee, "They say, 'Well, the cost per point in the market is $100. And we estimate that you're going to get a 10 rating. So that's going to be $1,000 a spot. Our show contains 30 spots, that's $30,000 a day, we're going to charge you half of that or $75,000 a week. You're going to make a 50 percent profit.' Well, there's a gap between the time you put the show on the air and you start selling—how much money really goes to the bottom line? Beware of this simplistic business approach; it's really not accurate."

- The price for programming is open to negotiation, regardless of what the other side would have you believe. Prices often have a direct relationship to the length of the license term. The more confident you are about the long-term success of a particular product, the more willing you should be to make an extended commitment in exchange for a lower fee. "It's a big risk," noted one broadcast manager, "but I think if you go for a two- or three- or four-year deal up front, you can get a very nice price break."

- Finally, let me present a tactic to support what some might term a "what's good for the goose is good for the gander" strategy. It was presented as both a suggestion and a wry observation by an astute manager. "Take a lesson from them. Syndicators by design do not close at your desk. They negotiate, you negotiate, and they get you to put your offer on the table. Pretty soon you say, 'Okay, let's write it up and I'll call the boss.' It's interesting. We never do that. I don't know why we don't."

As you can see, many of the recommendations are just refinements of the general principles discussed in the first chapter. These principles hold true in any type of negotiations, not just the three covered in this book. Review those principles. Reread that chapter and the more detailed exposition in Appendix A.

Conclusion

Broadcasters Can Negotiate Anything, as you have seen, is both the title of this book and a fact of life that reveals itself hundreds of times each day at stations large and small alike.

But having the ability to negotiate anything and consistently using that ability are two very different things indeed. Negotiation requires a continuing drive to stay in the best "shape" possible. Outstanding broadcast negotiators, some of whom have been interviewed specifically for this book, constantly strive to improve what they are doing by increasing their awareness of how they, their peers, and the other side negotiate.

These individuals also are interested in maintaining their negotiation skills over time, so that they can go on to the next battle with some added insight and with renewed motivation to succeed. From my experience, any program aimed at sharpening negotiating skills should build upon real-world experiences and recognize the role that plain, old-fashioned instinct plays in negotiation. A review of this book, it is hoped, will provide radio and television managers with a broader view of the negotiation process. How do both sides perceive a negotiation? How do other broadcasters react to situations that commonly arise? What is the current thinking on negotiation that is being generated by a growing number of negotiation experts? What are some practical ways to improve negotiation planning, strategies and tactics?

These questions are addressed here in-depth; the ultimate answers to any or all, of course, will evolve from your thoughts and actions in the various negotiation arenas that require your involvement. When all else is stripped away, remember that integrity is the real force behind every type of negotiation. By negotiating with a firm sense of purpose, you can bring profit and honor to all.

Appendix A: Effective Negotiating Styles

Effective Negotiators

What makes an effective negotiator? Survey research data by the Los Angeles-based Center for Effective Negotiating indicates that there are seven traits that those who negotiate for a living believe are most important: 1) planning skill; 2) an ability to think clearly under stress; 3) general practical intelligence; 4) verbal ability; 5) knowledge about the business; 6) personal integrity; and 7) an ability to perceive and exploit power.

Additional characteristics of effective negotiators were found in research conducted at the University of Southern California by the Center's president, Chester L. Karras (T.W. Crowell, 1970), They were:

- Negotiators who began with large initial demands improved their probability of success because they provided themselves with room to compromise later.
- Conversely, negotiators who made the largest initial concessions were likely to leave the negotiation with less than they wanted.
- Effective negotiators decreased rather than increased their concessions as a negotiation deadline approached.
- Skilled negotiators did not improve when they had more power, while unskilled negotiatiors did improve when they had more power.
- Skilled negotiators with power do not exploit it when dealing with unskilled negotiators.
- With equal power, the skill of the negotiator was a critical factor in determining the final outcome.
- Skilled negotiators are more likely to win very quick settlements than unskilled ones.

Before you decide if you possess these characteristics, we turn to a discussion of the negotiation process itself. Probably the most common questions that I am asked during my negotiation management training sessions are, "How do you know if the negotiation itself has been effective? How do broadcast managers and those that they negotiate with determine whether they have left the table with a satisfactory agreement?" The answers to these questions, in part, depend upon how negotiators perceive the negotiation process.

Competitive vs. Collaborative

There are two common strategies—or styles—of negotiation that dominate activities in the business world. They can be characterized as competitive or collaborative. The competitive negotiation closely follows the nature of competitive sporting events; one side wins and the other side loses. The collaborative strategy is based upon a Win-Win philosophy; a negotiation is successful only if all parties to it emerge as winners.

In a competitive negotiation, you consciously pursue your own goals at the expense of the other party. Given this, little or no trust is placed on their side, thus making it important to keep your cards close to your vest. You may also engage in misrepresentation or deception in order to keep the other side off balance. Competitive negotiations employ a variety of unpredictable actions that are designed to surprise and confuse the other side. Threats and bluffs are used to put the other side on the defensive and to maintain an upper hand. The name of the game is to identify the position of the opponent, then destroy it. This may involve ignoring logic and increasing the level of hostility to the other side. It may also create anxiety and fear on the other side, leading to concessions in response to your demands.

The collaborative style, in contrast, is designed to pursue goals that are held in common by both sides. There is an environment that encourages trust and openness in expressing thoughts and feelings, listening to each other, and actively exploring alternatives together. Both parties are in touch with their own needs and are willing to accurately represent them to the other side. The actions of both parties are not designed to create surprise. Collaboration involves treating each other with mutual understanding and integrity. The negotiation is characterized by using logical, creative and innovative processes to formulate workable solutions to common problems.

In competitive negotiations, both sides constantly work to dominate each other and exhibit little or no interest in what the other side has to say. There is a constant air of secrecy and frequent displays of irrational behavior by both sides. The end result is a Win-Lose situation. The loser feels a loss of self-esteem and also wishes to avoid responsibility for not "bringing home the bacon." The winner is viewed as an adversary, and the loser looks forward to the next encounter between them in order to even up the score.

Collaborative negotiations are designed to create Win-Win situations. Both parties accept solutions because they have been created legitimately within the negotiation itself, rather than outside it. As a result, they are happy to take responsibility for results and walk away from the table with enhanced self-esteem.

Transactional activities—buying and selling—create enormous temptations to engage in competitive negotiations. But in the broadcasting business, the manager should take a longer-term view. Reputations are a valuable form of currency. After a period of time, the manager cannot help but develop a list of who in the outside world plays fairly and who does not. As one manager commented during an interview, "We know who our friends are and we know who we think has given us less-than fair treatment in the past. And we're particularly leery of them."

Another manager commented, "There are people whom you can trust. They trust you. If you say, 'Hey, realistically this is all I can go,' they believe you. Or they say, 'This is my bottom line,' and you believe them." In short, broadcasting is a very people-oriented business. It depends upon long-standing relationships, and therefore requires nurturing them over time. The sporting analogy comes up short because the playing season never really ends.

The virtues of collaborative rather than competitive negotiations are articulated in different ways by those interviewed for this book. But to a person, every manager agreed that today's broadcast negotiation realities are too complex to engage in simplistic and often self-defeating Win-Lose negotiation activities.

Two comments of broadcast managers emphasize this point. One manager said, "You know, there's no deal until you both agree. To me, every deal is a good deal because it's good for both parties. As long as there is something of value for both sides, it's a good deal." Echoing the same idea, another manager stated, "a bad deal is when it is not fair for all parties.

When the thing is one way—my way—that's not necessarily fair to the other parties involved." I think these comments are representative of how broadcast managers approach negotiation in general.

Facilitating Collaborative Negotiations

Broadcast managers recognize the importance of their roles. They are different than stock speculators or commodities brokers. They are public figures in their communities and, in another sense, representatives of the industry as a whole. Broadcasts cannot deceive or dominate others in negotiations without losing credibility in the long term. A loss of credibility can lead to fewer vendors who are willing to deal with you and fewer sales prospects who are willing to return your telephone calls. Pursuing the goal of winning at all costs, in short, can be hazardous to your bottom line. For that reason alone, it is important to focus on how to facilitate collaborative negotiations as often as possible.

This task is often easier said than done. Broadcast managers thrive on competition. The marketplace is a measure of success in radio and television, and the more consistently you can beat out other stations in the market, the better you will look and the more money you will earn for your company.

Competition of this type is healthy. What becomes unhealthy is when the same competitive energy is brought into a negotiating room. There, your rival station is not likely to be present. Instead, you are negotiating with people or parties that can help give you a competitive advantage by providing you with more advertising sales, supporting research or better programming. It should be your goal to obtain these assets with the financial resources available to you, and to obtain them again and again in order to stay competitive.

That's one reason that Win-Win negotiations are so important. According to negotiating expert Herb Cohen, achieving mutual satisfaction through collaborative negotiation involves three major activities: 1) building trust; 2) gaining commitment; and 3) managing opposition.

Building trust requires an abandonment of the cynical view that people are inescapably evil or greedy. "In a *continuing relationship*," notes Cohen (Lyle Stewart, Seacaucus, NJ), "the more trust you place in others, the more they will justify your faith. Convey your belief in their honesty and reliability and you will encourage them to live up to these expectations." He counsels building trust on a continuing basis rather than trying to do so hastily during the heat of active bargaining. "Fortune will favor the person who uses his lead time to seed an environment of trust that will grow and ripen during the event.

This ability to use the present in anticipation of the future will make the difference. Before the conflict is formalized is when you can impact most effectively on the other side's attitude."

The process of gaining commitment recognizes the importance of those who influence the person or persons you are negotiating with. Herb Cohen cautions against viewing negotiators as isolated units. "See those whom you wish to persuade in context as a central core around which others move. Get the support of those others and you will influence the position and movement of the core."

The process of managing opposition involves encouraging shared ideas, information, experience and feelings in order to produce a mutually beneficial outcome. A common pitfall is to announce your position or "bottom line" since it will likely cause the other side to respond in kind. They may dig in their heels and express their own position as a demand or ultimatum. You then raise the stakes in response, and the negotiation veers off track as each side works to outdo the other. With each move they become further apart, and what began as a collaborative effort soon turns into a competitive one. The other side is transformed into an adversary, and the Win-Lose negotiating mode inevitably returns.

We have all been in situations where, despite building trust and gaining commitment by influencing others, the process breaks down because there is ineffective management of the other side. This is critical to keep in mind. Negotiation is a management process. Broadcast managers must bring to negotiation the full power of their managerial capabilities in order to achieve a "good outcome" in negotiations.

Successful Negotiations

What exactly is a "good outcome" and how can broadcasters aim at achieving it? As suggested above, neither shooting from the hip, playing "chicken" nor giving away the store is likely to generate the best result. For starters, broadcast managers should set their goals beyond simply achieving a deal that can be enforced, since a deal that makes poor business sense is likely to have little long-term value.

Broadcast managers must understand, articulate and refine their own goals and focus on what they want to achieve. Buying ratings services or programming for the lowest price and selling advertising time for the highest price are important goals, but they need not be the sole criteria by which to judge success. Other interests are involved. You may, for example, want to set a good precedent for other upcoming negotiations, or improve your image in the local business community.

Most people have a good sense of when they have been successful in a negotiation, but few analyze the criteria on which the conclusion has been based. Typical post-negotiation analyses might include questions such as these: "Who made the most concessions? Who ended up being pushed closer to their 'bottom line?' Who outlasted whom? Did I get everything they could offer?" A person's negotiating style is often a combination of techniques that have served him/her well in the past in arriving at one of these definitions of success.

Yet these measures of success in negotiation have serious drawbacks because they assume that negotiation is a contest of will. Haggling tends to reward stubbornness and deception. It can generate arbitrary outcomes; it can be time-consuming; and it may damage the relationship between the parties.

Professor Roger Fisher of the Harvard Law School is an authority on negotiation. In recent years, he and his colleagues at the Harvard Negotiation Project have developed an alternative set of working criteria for measuring a "good outcome" in negotiation. It may be helpful to consider the definition as a set of questions:

- Is the negotiated agreement better for all parties than what they could accomplish on their own without negotiation?
- Are our interests well satisfied? Are theirs acceptably satisfied (so that the agreement is durable)?
- Is the agreement one of the best possible options? Are all joint gains maximized? Are you certain there is no money "left on the table?"
- Is the agreement legitimate in the eyes of all parties? Are you certain no one feels "taken" and looks for revenge?
- Are the commitments made by the parties sufficient to solve the problem? Are they realistic and operational? Is everyone clear as to what happens next?
- Was the process—the way in which the agreement was reached—efficient? Was the agreement the product of good communication?
- Has the process of negotiating this agreement improved the working relationships among the parties? Will future negotiations be easier?

Obviously if you can answer "yes" to these questions, you have achieved an outstanding success in any given negotiation. Most of us, however, recall negotiation outcomes that fell short of this standard. This brings two questions to mind. First, why do we get less than optimal outcomes in negotiations? Second, how can we enhance negotiating power to maximize the chances of getting a better deal?

Negotiators, no matter what their style, make some common

errors. For example, parties involved in a negotiation pay a great deal of attention to the substance of the discussion. They are correct in doing so. An understanding of the facts (market data, projected operating costs), possible options and opportunities (technological breakthroughs, innovative business structures) and constraints (regulatory guidelines) is critical. Yet negotiators do not focus often enough on the process by which an agreement will be reached. They neglect to analyze the structure of the negotiation. They define "interested parties" too narrowly, not accounting for absent parties or groups which have ongoing interests but who have no representative at the table. They may not take the time to listen and gather information on the fundamental interests that underlie each party's position. They may not focus on how the parties, as people, are communicating.

Power in negotiation is not simply a function of resources, or the ability to inflict harm on the other side. Negotiation power lies in the ability to persuade others to agree to a solution that satisfies your interests. Your task is not to try and get them to say "yes" to a proposal that does not meet their needs. It is to invent an option that satisfies their interests acceptably, and then persuade them of its attractiveness and legitimacy. There is great power in being simultaneously firm and flexible, an advocate for your interests but open to persuasion. There is great power in basing offers and decisions on objective criteria.

Recommendations for Successful Negotiations

What is recommended? What will be useful to you tomorrow? These twelve prescriptive rules warrant consideration.

1. Clarifying Interests: Yours and Theirs. Your major interests in a negotiation are usually clear. You should clarify and articulate all other interests as well. The harder task is to understand the interests of the other parties at the table.

It is critical that you understand their choices, how they see them. For example, what if you walked into your station's door as a representative from Arbitron or Birch, or as a media buyer for an influential advertising agency? By putting yourself in the other side's position, you can better assess why they are resisting on a given issue. Listen, do your homework, gather information through sources available to you. Remember: they will not say "yes" to a proposal that doesn't meet their interests. Your task is to invent an option that meets your interests well, and theirs acceptably. Then persuade them that it is in their interest to accept it.

2. Avoid Feeling "Taken". Base offers and decisions on objective criteria. No one wants to feel that he gave in to pressure, that he wasn't as tough as he could have been, or that he was "taken." Likewise, you will not want to feel that you agreed to something that was not fair. Do some research. Analyze your station's own operating data, commission market research studies, gather sales and ratings information from other comparable markets. This information should then be used as a basis for advancing alternative approaches during negotiations. It is far easier for the other side to agree to a package that is founded on objective data and comparable precedent than to give in to an offer that comes out of thin air. Objective criteria are persuasive, and therefore powerful.

3. Separate the People from the Problem. As Roger Fisher and William Ury note in their book *Getting to Yes* (Houghton, Mifflin, 1981), "a basic fact about negotiation, easy to forget in corporate . . . transactions, is that you are dealing not with abstract representatives of the 'other side,' but with human beings. They have emotions, deeply held values, and different backgrounds and viewpoints; and they are unpredictable. So are you."

The heat of negotiation tempts us to forget this basic principle. The problems and obstacles to agreement surface early on, and we project onto those we are negotiating with all of these complex issues. Problems and people become intertwined, and soon people are relating to each other at a different level, one that labels each person as a "good guy" or "bad guy." But as we know, nothing is that simple.

Force yourself to deal with the other side as people while simultaneously dealing with the negotiation problems at hand. Each individual on the other side has a complex combination of personal and corporate needs that require identification and response.

One useful way to sort out these needs and develop tactics for dealing with them during a negotiation is to analyze them in terms of the Maslow Triangle. The Maslow Triangle, also known as the Maslow Hierarchy of Needs, was first presented by psychologist Abraham Maslow in 1954. In the book, *Motivation and Personality*, Maslow said that people organize their needs by ranking them from most to least important. Since in most cases not all needs can be satisfied, we seek to have as many as possible fulfilled in negotiation, in order of importance. The most important needs are the most basic: those related to *survival*. Once physiological needs are fulfilled, we seek out *safety* in the form of protection, comfort and predictability. Next, as social creatures, we look for affection and acceptance—a sense of *belonging*. We then move on to look for some measure of *worth*, which may be money, power or prestige. Finally, we seek to achieve *self-actualization*, a high state of self-esteem and internal balance.

According to Chester L. Karras in his book *The Negotiating Game* (T.W. Crowell, 1970), all negotiations should take this hierarchy of needs into account. You should work at satisfying lower-level needs first, then move upward to satisfy higher needs. In other words, people seek to create harmony between their personal values and those of their business. Negotiators who keep this in mind will gain new insights into those sitting on the opposite side of the table.

The process of separating people from the problem is often difficult to accomplish because of the way a negotiation may begin. Due in large part to our competitve instincts, we tend to move too quickly toward positional bargaining. Each side works out a position or series of positions in advance, argues for it with the other side, then demonstrates a willingness to make concessions in order to reach a compromise agreement. Both sides may in fact walk away with something, but they do so grumbling under their breath that it's not really what they wanted.

Broadcast negotiators can achieve more if they break out of this ritualistic behavior by not basing a negotiation outcome on an exchange of positions. As Fisher and Ury (Houghton, Mifflin, 1981) note,

> "When negotiators bargain over positions, they tend to lock themselves into those positions. The more you clarify your position and defend it against attack, the more committed you become to it. The more you try to convince the other side of the impossibility of changing your opening position, the more difficult it becomes to do so. Your ego becomes identified with your position. . . ."

> "As more attention is paid to positions, less attention is devoted to meeting the underlying concerns of the parties. Agreement becomes less likely. Any agreement reached may reflect a mechanical splitting of the difference between final solutions rather than a solution carefully crafted to meet the legitimate interests of the parties. The result is frequently an agreement less satisfactory to each side than it could have been."

Rejecting positional bargaining doesn't mean you should become a pushover, either. Leo Durocher's famous phrase, "Nice Guys Finish Last," has enough truth in it to serve as a warning against bending over backwards in the other direction. The danger in being a "soft" positional negotiator is in being taken advantage of by someone who takes a hard line. Since positional bargaining is part of the Win-Lose mentality, the person who demands, deceives and threatens the best is likely to emerge victorious.

By changing the rules at the outset, you can redefine the negotiation game you are playing and therefore can be more in control of helping to produce a good outcome.

4. Focus on What Your Interests Really Are. Positional bargaining is centered on external indicators that we are willing to reveal to the other side. The problem with stating our position, no matter how sincere it is, is that the other side will always tend to distrust it because the ground rules call for secrecy, bluffing and the like. Moreover, your position may obscure other related issues, creating a likelihood that they will be left unresolved during a negotiation.

For example, your position may be buying a ratings service or syndicated program package for x dollars (and not one cent more). But your interest may be to obtain better service from the vendor, which may include such concerns as low current price, price stability, responsiveness to complaints and receiving advance notice of new services or programs. It is not necessary to lay out all of these interests at once. But it is important that your planning process account for the full range of concerns you have that are capable of resolution between the other party and yourself. Similarly, if the other side opens with a statement of position, you should begin to probe what interests are being served by the position, and if other interests remain unaddressed because they have been overshadowed by the drive to achive a "bottom line" in negotiation. The concept of a bottom line should be left to assessing your company's overall financial performance rather than as the litmus test for determining whether any particular negotiation has been successful.

5. Understand Options. A critical element of negotiation planning should be assessing what you will do if you cannot reach agreement with the other side. One pitfall to watch for is feeling compelled to reach an agreement, even if the terms are unsatisfactory, because you have invested so much time and energy in the negotiation process itself. In order to avoid this, and in order to enhance your power in a negotiation, you should focus on a different scenario—namely, what alternatives do you have if you don't reach agreement with the other side. With some creative thinking, you will often find that you have a number of options available, some of which you have not thought of before. For advertising sales, you may be able to pursue a broader base of sponsors. For radio ratings services, you may be able to strengthen your in-house research capabilities. For syndicated television programming, you may find that your schedule can accomodate a talk show as well as a game show as the lead-in to your early news.

Radio and television stations are dynamic organizations, and many among your staff would be more than happy to suggest options that they perceive in their day-to-day activities. By devoting sufficient attention to how you would proceed if the negotiation never took place, you can instill a new level of confidence in your ability to probe strengths and weaknesses once you sit down at the negotiating table.

On the other side, it is important to understand what their options may be. What happens if they go across the street to a rival station? Will they be in a stronger or weaker position selling or buying from someone else if it becomes known that they were not able to reach agreement with your station? And how will this affect their dealings in other markets?

Once you analyze options on both sides, it is important to develop a strategy that maximizes your alternatives while minimizing theirs. The more options that you have outside the negotiation, and the fewer they have, the greater the likelihood that both sides will want to reaching an agreement or that you will be better off walking away rather than reaching any agreement at all.

6. Establish A Realistic Aspiration Level. Drawing upon a review of experiments designed to determine characteristics of underachievers in school as well as data from original research, Chester L. Karras, *The Negotiation Game* (T.W. Carroll, 1970), concluded that there is a growing body of evidence indicating that those with high aspirations in the context of negotiation are more likely to reach higher goals than those who do not.

Those who emphasize success are likely to overestimate what can be achieved in a negotiation, while those who fear failure take a more pessimistic view. Equally important, the fear of failure can produce a lowered level of expectations about what you will be able to achieve during a negotiation. After all, the less you expect, the less likely you will feel failure if you do not achieve the goal.

Although these findings suggest that pessimism can create unsatisfactory, self-fulfilling results, they also show that the other extreme can be equally damaging. As Chester Karras, *The Negotiation Game* (T.W. Carrol, 1970), notes, "It's good to have high aspirations, but it's not good if they are so high as to be unrealistic." The lesson to be learned here is that it is important to set high yet realistic aspiration levels rather than set lower ones in order to reduce the possibility of failure. Moreover, when delegating negotiating authority, it is critical to articulate the aspiration level you want to be brought to the table. All too often, this is not done. Management merely says "Do the best you can" without confiming that the person representing you will be as confident and assertive as you think would be appropriate in a given situation.

7. Make Strategic Use of Information. Good negotiation outcomes flow from good information accepted as credible by both sides. Therefore, your task should be to develop as much information as possible in your planning activities. This information should be persuasive not just to the other side, but also to a disinterested mediator if one were brought in to facilitate a decision by both sides. Information is a great source of power in negotiations; conversely, a lack of information is likely to be used against you at critical points.

The key point in developing information is that it be accepted as objective. The most persuasive information is often that which the other side already has in hand and accepts as valid, such as information from respected trade publications or research firms.

Relying on information in negotiations also allows you to argue strongly without diverting the discussion to one that centers on personality differences. Differences can still exist, but they should be on the basis of something that can be verified or tested in some other way rather than on subjective, abstract impressions.

Information should encompass a broad range of criteria that is capable of being accepted as a fair standard. It should include such indicators as cost, market value, efficiency and precedent. Moreover, it is important to look beyond the information in order to determine whether it was gathered in a fair manner.

Two other related points deserve emphasis. First, a Win-Win negotiation should frame each issue as a collective search for objective criteria. Second, you should seek to reason which standards for information are most appropriate and how they should be applied. Always ask, "How was this standard arrive at?," both for your information and theirs. Agreement on standards for decisions should be discussed during the negotiation and should be settled before you proceed to discuss terms. In practice, the reverse is typically the case. In the rush to discuss terms, parties too often ignore the realization that it is unlikely that terms can ever be agreed upon if both sides have not agreed what criteria will be used to reach a decision.

8. Encourage Creative Thinking. One drawback in emphasizing the importance of "doing your homework" prior to a negotiation is that managers may take this advice too literally. Negotiation is a dynamic process. Although pre-negotiation planning is essential, it should not be perceived as carving matters into stone. In practice, most creative thinking about options will come during meetings between your side and theirs.

As Roger Fisher and William Ury explain in their best-selling book *Getting to Yes* (Houghton-Mifflin, 1981), "In most negotiations there are four major obstacles that inhibit the inventing of an abundance of options: 1) premature judgment; 2) searching for the single answer; 3) the assumption of a fixed pie; and 4) thinking that solving their problem is their problem."

Most negotiators are too result-oriented at the outset, which can create a distorted view of the overall picture. By seeking to reach a decision too quickly, they run the risk of closing off discussion on a large number of possibilities that may lead to a more satisfactory outcome. Saying this is the "bottom line" of what you will pay may sound impressive, but it also may not reflect a more complex set of concerns that you thought about before you came up with a dollar figure that embodies them.

9. Do Not Yield to Pressure. You may find yourself in a negotiation where subtle or overt pressure is applied to you in order to reach agreement. Such pressure frequently is caused by time constraints, such as the necessity for booking ad sales for the coming quarter or syndicated programming for next season. The failure to set a mutual agenda at the beginning of in-person negotiating often creates different perceptions about how much time the parties anticipate is needed to reach agreement. With the caveat that everything takes considerably more time than anticipated, you should establish a realistic timetable that accounts for time to review information, to consult with others, and to develop counterproposals. Without such a timetable, you are likely to be pressured into reaching an agreement that may be a bad outcome, or to pressure the other side into entering an agreement that they may not honor later. Regardless of how quickly a decision must be made, you always can create a more reasonable timetable by beginning the negotiation process at an earlier date.

There are other pressures that arise during the negotiation which may cause you to rethink what you want to achieve. You may be threatened or confronted with what seems like an unmovable force on the other side. You may be pressured by someone trying to manipulate your emotions by questioning whether you really trust them, which is a tangential issue at best.

Do not yield to any of these tactics. Stand your ground by suggesting what objective criteria you think should apply (and why), and by asking the other side to explain its reasoning about the objective criteria it favors. At the least, this approach will keep the discussion based on the merits and will force the other side to move in this direction if it wants to advance its interests.

10. Don't Be A Disembodied Negotiator. The telephone is a crucial piece of technology that broadcast managers utilize to convey and receive information and advice from people inside and outside their company. The ability to use the telephone effectively is a tremendous asset for a manager, and one that should be employed without a second thought in order to facilitate the process of disseminating and gathering information.

On the other hand, broadcast managers too often overutilize the telephone in negotiations. They extend its use beyond negotiation planning to make it serve as a convenient substitute for face-to-face contact.

Agreements are best reached through the give-and-take of an open, in-person discussion. This allows both parties to build a relationship based upon something more than a disembodied voice on the line. Telephone calls and letters are useful to follow up on issues, but the negotiation process should emphasize in person contacts as well.

One frequent area of concern is what effect the location of a negotiation meeting may have on the outcome. Based again on the historic linkage between negotiation and sports competition, conventional wisdom says that one way to gain the upper hand in any negotiation is to choose the home field advantage. Although there may be some slight psychological advantage in this, the more important aspect to focus on is how to use location as an advantage regardless of where you negotiate.

If the meeting takes place at your offices, you can exert control over administrative details and have ready access to any internal resource that you need to clarify a negotiating point, such as what you paid for comparable syndicated programming from the same supplier. Your staff and its files are likely to be but a short distance away. Additionally, the other side may be willing to make concessions based on their travel schedule rather than on the merits being discussed.

Home-field advantage has drawbacks as well. First, it makes it more difficult to delay, since the other side knows that the information you need is more readily available. Second, it may lead the other side to delay matters by saying it needs to return to its home office for further approval, a situation that arises frequently when you express a willingness to buy.

Negotiating on the other side's turf frequently can be as advantageous, if not more so. First, if you initiate the suggestion that meetings take place there, it can create an impression that you feel confident about the information and arguments on your side, which in itself may be a psychological advantage. Second, you can ask to meet with higher authority or for the other side to check on uncertain facts and in doing so, blunt any delaying tactics.

Those wary of favoring either location may opt for a neutral site. This seems good in theory, but it may be unproductive due to an inability by either side to call experts and supporting data at will. Negotiation is a complex enough process; unless there is a compelling reason, try to meet on familiar ground to at least one side. If a compromise is necessary, alternate meetings between your offices and theirs.

11. Be A Good Listener. At its core, negotiation is a communications process. Negotiators frequently conclude that, accordingly, they will be most effective by taking the lead in discussions in order to make sure their positions are understood by the other side. Although the desire for clarity is admirable, it may put too much emphasis on speaking rather than listening.

According to negotiating expert Gerard Nierenberg (Nierenberg & Zief, New York), "listening is as much a persuasive technique as speaking. A successful listener must keep an open mind and strive to be free from bias and preconceived notions." Listening builds trust between parties and shows respect for the other side's ideas. It also provides you with a period to process information and formulate follow-up questions.

A negotiation is not a debate. Listening need not be followed by an immediate response for every point that the other side raises. It is also important to listen to questions asked of you before responding. There is a tendency among some people to interrupt questions with answers in order to preempt discussion. Such a technique is discourteous and counterproductive to advancing the negotiation itself. If you are unclear about the question, ask the other side to repeat it, or to rephrase the question in other words.

Listening encompasses more than hearing the words of someone else. Conversation is accompanied by a variety of vocal inflections and nonverbal cues, commonly called "body language." It is important to be tuned into these since they can convey many shades of meaning about what is being said. And keep in mind that your own nonverbal responses that accompany listening will send signals to the other side, too. Be aware of your body language so that the messages you send while listening are those that you intend.

12. Exhibit a Sense of Humor. Broadcast negotiations are serious business. Typically, substantial dollar amounts are at issue in purchase and sales transactions. Personal and professional reputations are often on the line. That does not mean that you have to leave your sense of humor behind.

Negotiating authorities Henry H. Calero and Bob Oskam note that "humor works like nothing else to help keep or put things in manageable perspective." A bit of humor, used purposely, is appropriate during a negotiation and can be used to create strategic advantages that favor your side as well. It can be used to attract the other side's attention to your point, or to maintain interest during a long discussion.

Humor also can be utilized to emphasize a point that you want the other side to remember. The best way to accomplish this is through a maxim or anecdote that is on point with what you want to communicate. Humor is a good way to break tension that is often apparent during a negotiation, especially if it is unexpected. Try it once or twice, but don't keep repeating the pattern so as much as become predictable.

Any humor used in a negotiation should be good-natured and not aimed at getting a laugh at the expense of any participant. Sarcastic or insulting humor, or off-color jokes, can poison a negotiation by offending someone else's sensibilities, and you should be careful to avoid making remarks of this nature. Humor also should not be used solely for the purpose of ingratiating yourself with the other side. After all, building a good working relationship does not mean that you must also emerge as the most popular or likable negotiator.

Be receptive to humor from the other side. A sense of humor involves being able to appreciate a good joke as well as tell one. Acknowledging the other side's sense of humor can send a powerful message about how much you value the other side's participation, which in turn can promote better communication regarding the more serious issues at hand.

Negotiating Bibliography

The books below are recommended for further reference on negotiation and related processes.

Axelrod, R., *The Evolution of Cooperation*, Basic Books: New York, 1985.

Calero, H. and Oskam, B., *Negotiate the Deal You Want*, Dodd: New York, 1983.

Cohen, H., *You Can Negotiate Anything*, Lyle Stuart: Seacaucus, NJ, 1980.

Fisher, R., and Ury, W., *Getting to YES*, Houghton-Mifflin: Boston, 1981.

Karrass, C., *The Negotiating Game: How To Get What You Want*, T. Y. Crowell: New York, 1970.

Karrass, C., *Give and Take: The Complete Guide to Negotiating Strategies and Tactics*, T. Y. Crowell: New York, 1974.

Lax, D. and Sebenius, J., *The Manager as Negotiator*, Free Press: 1986.

Lewicki, R., and Litterer, J., *Negotiation*, Irwin: Homewood, IL, 1985.

Morrison, W., *The Pre-Negotiation Planning Book*, Wiley & Sons, Inc.: New York, 1985.

Nierenberg, G., *The Art of Negotiating*, Pocket Books: New York, 1984.

Nierenberg, G., *The Complete Negotiator*, Nierenberg & Zief: New York, 1986.

Nierenberg, G., *Fundamentals of Negotiating*, Harper & Row: New York, 1987.

Pruitt, D., *Negotiation Behavior*, Academic Press: San Diego, 1981.

Raiffa, H., *The Art and Science of Negotiation*, Harvard Univ. Press: Cambridge, 1985.

Warschaw, T., *Winning by Negotiation*, Berkley Pub.: New York, 1981.

Zartman, I.W., *The Practical Negotiator*, Yale Univ. Press: New Haven, 1982.

Appendix B: Negotiation Planning, Execution and Review

"In the real world," according to negotiation expert William Morrison, "thousands of people are negotiating every day, and most of these people are not very successful because they do not do a complete planning job. They do not invest the time. They do not believe it is necessary. Planning will typically take more effort than the actual negotiation and will vary in time based upon the negotiation, but it is essential."

Introduction

What are the risks that poor negotiation planning usually create? Quite simply, if your side is not prepared to negotiate an issue and the other side is, it will be extremely unlikely that your side will be able to prevail on that issue. As to benefits, the more attention you devote to negotiation issues and concerns in advance, the more comfortable and assured you will be when the negotiation actually begins. You will have a clear understanding of what you want to achieve and what can be achieved through a successful negotiation. You will also be aware of available options if and when the negotiation does not lead to an agreement. You will be in a position to learn from your experiences and to build upon them so that successful negotiating becomes a continuous pattern rather than a random event.

This section presents a detailed, step-by-step process for planning, executing and evaluating a negotiation. It is based upon the author's extensive background in advising broadcast managers on negotiation issues. The materials here have been used in actual negotiations on numerous occasions, and with overwhelmingly successful results.

In fairness, even the most inexperienced negotiator tends to devote some attention to pre-negotiation planning. Their results—or more often lack of results—stem from not planning properly, not perceiving the "lay of the land" before the journey begins. The planning framework here seeks to correct this by leading you, the user, through a sequence of steps that are designed to let you play to your strengths, and to spot and correct weaknesses before the other side takes advantage of them.

Based upon experience, it seems that many negotiations are doomed to fail well before either side gets to the first meeting. The reason is poor negotiation planning—a failure to consider all the issues that might arise; a failure to anticipate how the other side perceives these issues; and a failure to articulate negotiation priorities, strategies and tactics.

The words of several leading broadcasting negotiators bear highlighting here to provide insight about how important they view the negotiation *planning* process.

> I've never been in a negotiation that I didn't plan out personally—every move, every possible objection that may come up on the other side and every side step. You don't walk in with just one flat idea. That's like walking into a room with no back doors.

You have to know where you're going. It's like getting in your automobile and heading for the West Coast. How do you get there? Eventually you'll get there. It helps a lot if you sit down and look at the road map and find out what's in the best interests of all parties concerned. Then, through discussion, try to reach that goal.

Before I go into any negotiation, I list all of the things in the process of making the agenda: various outcomes and various things that can happen. It gives me much more flexibility. I isolate what I'm willing to give up and what I want. Some of the things at the bottom of the list I'm willing to use as a chip in negotiation to get back some of the things that are important at the top of the list.

I've sold off the top of my head with handshake deals, at one-fourth of what the going rate was. I had to tell my salesman that I had to stick to that mistake because I couldn't go back and tell the other guy about my problem. And so I had to eat three quarters of the actual cost because I low-balled him, because I didn't have the thing written down in front of me.

In any negotiation that you go into on the retail level, you have a great advantage if you know the parameters. If you want $10,000 and you're willing to accept $8,000, or on the other hand if you're buying programming or products of some kind and you're willing to pay $6,000 if you know that—the other side doesn't know that, so you have a great advantage.

I think when you go into a negotiation, you've got to decide in the beginning what you want in the end or you're really subject to pressure. Eliminate the pressure on yourself by knowing what you want to have happen and where the line is drawn. Then you won't just be blowing in the wind as you get pressure from various sources.

In any negotiation, I think we have got to do a far better job than we're doing of determining what is our goal, what is our objective. What do I have to do to put all the pieces together to meet that goal?

Objectives of Planning

Your side, their side: good negotiation planning will account for both. The worksheets included at the end of this section are intended to have you look inward to your own company and your own personal needs within it. They are also intended to have you look outward, to put yourself in the position of those on the other side. Without such a dual approach, negotiation planning would take place in a vacuum. Negotiation by definition is a process with at least two parties; you must always be sensitive to what the other side wants to achieve and be aware of how it is trying to achieve it.

Outside of negotiation, we see the beneficial effects of planning at many levels. The greatest chess masters or tournament bridge players are characterized not for their sleight of hand or deft moves at the table. They separate themselves from the pack by their ability to plan out their moves in advance. They anticipate what will happen when the game begins, and improve their play by continually reviewing what has worked and what has not. The same can be said for the most successful military strategists, football coaches, or trial lawyers. With little if any exception, virtually all professionals regardless of their field share a common attribute for success—planning.

Effective negotiation planning need not be a series of activities designed to overload busy radio and television managers with information or additional obligations. Rather, negotiation planning works best when it is accepted as part of the seamless web of ongoing station operations. Conversely, if negotiation planning is approached as a series of activities to be performed in isolation, the most likely outcome will be an understandable sense of annoyance.

Every negotiation should be preceded by a restatement of what you want to achieve. If the goals of the negotiation cannot be summarized in a sentence or two, the parties are likely to drift away from central concerns to ones that are tangential or even irrelevant. With an upcoming negotiation, there may be a tendency to have all issues that relate to your side and theirs resolved at once. The danger of this approach is that too much is piled on the plate, leaving no one in a position to digest anything.

Negotiations work best when they are focused on a small number of related issues. As a general proposition, I have found that dealing with more than *seven* issues simultaneously, regardless of their close connection, is a step down the road leading to counterproductive results. Each worksheet, accordingly, is formatted to include no more than seven issues at a time. If more than this number arises, be prepared for a mental warning signal to go off.

Negotiation planning is not an end in itself. It is part and parcel of implementing a workable agreement aimed at improving your station's operations and ultimately, your bottom line. Even the most meticulously-completed set of worksheets are meaningless if they are not used to achieve measurable results. In other words, always undertake negotiation planning in order to reach a decision that will be workable in practice.

The notion of negotiation planning carries with it the danger of conveying the same amount of awe in the broadcast manager's mind as the notion of infinity. "It's too long and complex," this line of reasoning goes, "and besides, I don't know where to begin."

The worksheets in this book demonstrate that effective negotiation planning can be broken down into many smaller parts. No matter how big the problem at hand, or how far ahead one must forecast, it is possible to approach the negotiation with a series of modest planning steps that are easy to manage.

The role of the broadcast manager is to provide vision and leadership within his or her company. Too often, though, managers mistake this charge as a directive to act like the Lone Ranger when negotiations take place. A better alternative is to create an environment that encourages collaboration in negotiation planning.

Perceptions are often as important as realities in negotiation. Within limits, the more different perceptions you can incorporate into negotiation planning, the fuller picture you are likely to have. Subordinates and peers from other parts of your organization thus should be viewed as valued team members with specialized information and expertise to contribute.

Staff Involvement in Negotiation Planning

Negotiation planning should always involve the highest levels of management in your company, at the least, in the role of overseer. The individuals responsible for the actual negotiation, of course, should have the greatest involvement in planning and review. They are the closest to the action, and will have the greatest impact on the final outcome. The worksheets will aid your ability to track delegated activities as well as manage directly the negotiation activities that are central to your job responsibilities.

Review with your staff in terms of its assets in negotiation planning and implementation. One way to accomplish this is by compiling a company-wide "talent bank" that categorizes how key employees contribute to negotiations. If this is done, the information will be readily available to assist you in assembling an "A-Team" for any particular negotiation that arises. Where appropriate, do not be afraid to augment this team with outside resources that can help you save time, provide another level of expertise, function objectively as a "third eye," ask critical questions that may be uncomfortable for those within a company to raise, or play the role of "devil's advocate" for the other side.

Pre-negotiation planning should be characterized by promoting a free flow of information within your organization. Those involved in the process should be encouraged to exchange their ideas verbally or in writing. Information that may be particularly useful includes background sketches of other companies and personalities that will be involved in the negotiation. Additionally, your staff may have new or additional information regarding how the competition in your market, or those in comparable markets, have dealt with these same players. Your staff should be reminded about the importance of maintaining the confidentiality about this information, and about disciplinary measures that may be implemented if leaks occur.

Aside from improving the negotiation outcome itself, the team approach can enhance the overall morale of your staff. Negotiating is a central part of any station's activities, and giving staffers a real sense of being part of that process will encourage them to keep their eyes and ears open for information that may be useful to future negotiations.

Use of Worksheets

The worksheets, in short, are designed to assist you in 1) pre-negotiation planning, 2) the negotiation itself, and 3) post-negotiation review. They are intended to help you discuss negotiations with staff so that all involved share common goals. These worksheets need not be filled out every time your station sells commercial time, for example, but they may be useful in assessing how your ongoing sales program can be improved. Alternatively, briefly reviewing some of these worksheets prior to a negotiation will focus your attention on the upcoming negotiation. Or you may find completely some, or all, of the worksheets to be useful when a major negotiation—such as with a radio ratings service or television program syndicator—looms ahead. In other words, use them as you best see fit and use them to achieve better negotiation outcomes over time.

The worksheets are set up so that the major issues raised by the worksheets precede the actual worksheet. Consider these issues and let the worksheet lead you along to evaluate these issues.

Negotiating Worksheets

Negotiation: Worksheet 1

What Do You Wish to Accomplish From The Negotiation?

How Will It Serve the Long-Term Interests of Your Company and Your Position Within It?

What Specific Outcomes Would be Acceptable to Achieve These Goals?

1. Negotiation Goals and Desired Outcome

- Imagine that your upcoming negotiation has already concluded, and you are writing with the benefit of 20/20 hindsight. How would you describe what you sought to accomplish? Did it serve the long-term interests of your company and your position within it?

- With your goals articulated, continue by describing the successful outcome that the negotiation achieved. Taken together, these descriptions can serve as a benchmark for where you want events to lead. The saying, "If you don't know where you're going, any road will take you there," bears repeating here as a reminder that a negotiation can never be successful if criteria for evaluating it are not established at the outset.

Negotiation Goals

1.

2.

3.

Negotiation Outcomes

1.

2.

3.

Negotiation: Worksheet 2

In negotiation, as in many other areas, timing frequently determines how an issue is resolved. Therefore, it is important at the outset to define when, and in some cases, how long each phase of the negotiation process will take. This worksheet establishes benchmarks that, taken together, can be charted along a Time Line to create a realistic assessment of when an agreement can be expected.

2. Negotiation Timetable

This negotiation timetable is presented in reverse order in order for you to create a backtiming sequence.

- Anticipated Duration of Negotiation

- Date Agreement Must Be Finalized

- Date Decision Must Be Made by Final Authority

- Date Initial Decision Must Be Made

- Date First Negotiation Session Will Be Held

- Date Supporting Information Will Be Gathered

- Date Negotiation Planning Will Begin

Negotiation: Worksheet 3

With goals, desired outcomes and timing in mind, the next step is to identify the issues that will be in the negotiation, and who will raise them if they are brought up by your side. This worksheet emphasizes the importance of establishing an order or priority for negotiation issues and of limiting them to a workable number. Even if there seems to be only one issue (e.g., price), there probably are additional issues that flow from it. Put another way, if your highest priority issue was resolved, what additional elements would have to be addressed in order for the negotiation to be completed?

3. Negotiation Issues: Your Side

- List each anticipated issue in the negotiation in order of priorities to you. Assign a value to each issue on a scale of 1-10 (10 being the most important, 1 being the least important).

- If you anticipate this issue will be brought up by your side during the negotiation, indicate the name of the person who will raise it.

Issue	Importance Value:	To Be Brought Up By

1.

2.

3.

4.

5.

6.

7.

Negotiation: Worksheet 4

This worksheet is the first step in your task of viewing the negotiation from the other side's vantage point. There may be more than one other side, of course, so it will be important to complete an additional worksheet of this type for every side. As with the prior worksheet, this worksheet is designed to help you get all the issues out on the table. It follows the rank order approach and, like the other worksheet, instructs you to assign a numerical importance value to each issue in order to make the task of prioritizing an easier one. Anticipating who will bring these issues up is also important, and appropriate space is provided to complete this information.

4. Negotiation Issues: Their Side

List each anticipated issue in the negotiation in order of importance to the other side. Assign a value to each issue on a scale of 1-10 (10 being the most important, 1 being the least important).

Issue   **Importance Value:**

1.

2.

3.

4.

5.

6.

7.

Negotiation: Worksheet 5

It is useful to compare both lists after completing them to see any differences and to evaluate priorities for each side. Comparing them will also help in developing a strategy for raising an issue or responding to one. For example, it might be appropriate to raise one of their issues first in order to indicate your preparedness and your willingness to deal with all reasonable concerns. Or it may be useful to raise an issue of lesser importance first if it is given a higher priority on the other side. This worksheet allows you to consolidate information from the previous two worksheets in order to pursue comparisons in an efficient manner.

5. Consolidated Issues Worksheet

Issue	Importance Value: Your Side	Importance Value: Their Side

1.

2.

3.

4.

5.

6.

7.

8.

9.

10.

11.

12.

13.

14.

Negotiation: Worksheet 6

Now that you have assessed what issues are likely to be included in the negotiation, it is important to shift your focus to issues that your side wishes to have excluded. Here again, it is important to list these issues in rank order and to assign an importance value on a 1-10 scale for each. Because issues tend to creep into a negotiation if there is a remote connection to other issues, it is important to note a "best response" that could be raised if the other side questioned why the issue was not being included. The worksheet is designed to cover both your side and their side. As to the latter, you should anticipate the issues that the other side wishes to exclude, in rank order of importance for exclusion. The "best response" inquiry should also be made—namely, how would their side respond if the issue was raised by your side? What would they say to persuade you that it not be addressed during the negotiation? Given the consolidated nature of this worksheet, you will be able to compare information for each side for use in later strategic and tactical planning.

6. Issues to be Excluded

- List the issues you wish to exclude from the negotiation, and those you anticipate their side wishes to exclude. These should be in order of which issues are most important to avoid, and a value from 1-10 (10 being the most important, 1 being the least) should be assigned for each issue.

- If one or more of these issues is raised, what will be the best response to ensure that they are taken out of the negotiation? The best responses for both your side and their side should be indicated in the appropriate space.

- If an issue to be excluded creeps into the negotiation despite a best response, what other issues is it likely to have an impact on? These other issues, which should have been identified already, should be indicated in the appropriate space.

	Issue/Your Side	Importance Value	Best Response	Issues to be Impacted
1.				
2.				
3.				
4.				
5.				
6.				
7.				

6. Issues to be Excluded *(continued)*

	Issue/Their Side	Importance Value	Best Response	Issues to be Impacted
1.				
2.				
3.				
4.				
5.				
6.				
7.				

Negotiation: Worksheet 7

This worksheet is designed to allow the compilation of information about the chain of command for decisionmaking authority that exists on both sides. It is intended to generate a specific understanding of who is empowered to make an agreement, and the dollar amount they are authorized to approve. For group ownership situations, the chain of command may extend beyond station boundaries to other corporate offices. Knowledge of this, too, will be useful in identifying who is necessary to achieve agreement.

7. Negotiation Authority

- It is important to identify the level of authority for each person on your side and each person on their side. In effect, this establishes a chain of command and a recognition of the limitations that may be present at a meeting. Where contracting authority is at issue, also indicate the dollar amount that each individual can authorize.

Your Side	Individual	Title	Authority	Dollar Amount Level of Authorization
1.				
2.				
3.				
4.				
5.				
6.				
7.				

Worksheets

7. Negotiation Authority *(continued)*

Their Side	Individual	Title	Authority	Dollar Amount Level of Authorization
1.				
2.				
3.				
4.				
5.				
6.				
7.				

Negotiation: Worksheet 8

Information is power. Information is the fuel of negotiation. Information is a tool to persuade, justify and achieve commitments. Information is also a random commodity. If it is not organized with a specific purpose in mind, information loses much of its usefulness, perhaps all of it. This worksheet is designed to shape information to the specific issues that you will be addressing in the negotiation. The more you can introduce objective and verifiable information to support an issue (or refute one), the greater the likelihood that your argument will be credible to the other side. Additionally, it is important to know where each piece of supporting information is filed so that it can be retrieved as necessary. Better yet, as each document is located, it should be duplicated for a standalone negotiation file that is indexed according to issue. Finally, as a check for usefulness, the worksheet requests that you indicate why this information is relevant. If your confidence about its relevance is brought into question, this should raise a red flag regarding that specific piece of information which you intend to use.

8. Information Gathering: Your Side

- This worksheet should be used to identify information gathered to support an issue to be raised by your side during the negotiation. Transfer the issues from the "Negotiation Issues: Your Side" worksheet. Then indicate what information will be used to support you in advancing the issue, where it can be found in your organization and why the information is relevant.

Issue	Supporting Information	Where It Is	Relevance
1.			
2.			
3.			
4.			
5.			
6.			
7.			

Negotiation: Worksheet 9

One pitfall in analyzing information for negotiation purposes is not taking into account what information their side presents to support or refute various issues. Evaluating their information as you become aware of it (whether before or during a negotiation) is essential so that you can determine where it came from, if it differs from yours and if it is timely or outdated. Sufficient space is provided here so that you can note these differences for comparison.

9. Information Evaluation: Their Side

- This worksheet should be used to evaluate information that is presented by their side to support or refute an issue during a negotiation. List information that is presented by their side and indicate its timeliness (i.e., how old the information is). If your information is significantly different, indicate the source of your information and how it differs from theirs.

Issue	Timeliness	Source of Differing Information	What Differing Information Says
1.			
2.			
3.			
4.			
5.			
6.			
7.			

Negotiation: Worksheet 10

For each issue listed in rank order by importance value, you should briefly indicate which company need is satisfied by a successful resolution of the issue. The five categories are 1) short-term financial (cash flow); 2) long-term financial (revenue growth and profits); 3) marketing (business image); 4) human resources (company morale); and 5) continued relations with outside vendors (external stability). More than one need may be listed, as may others that are important but otherwise not categorized.

10. *Analyzing Company Needs: Your Side*

- List each issue of the negotiation in order of importance and assign a value (10 being the most important, 1 being the least important).

- Indicate which company needs a successful resolution of the issue would satisfy. The five categories to be used here are 1) short-term financial (cash flow); 2) long-term financial (revenue growth and profits); 3) marketing (business image); 4) human resources (company morale); and 5) continued relations with outside vendors (external stability). More than one need may be listed.

Issue	Importance Value	Need(s)
1.		
2.		
3.		
4.		
5.		
6.		
7.		

Negotiation: Worksheet 11

This worksheet mirrors the prior one and is intended to focus your attention on the other side's company needs. Here, it may be useful to review company literature, trade press clippings, and public filings made by their side to ascertain with some accuracy what their motivations are as a company.

11. Analyzing Company Needs: Their Side

- List the issues of the negotiation in order of importance and assign a value for each (10 being the most important, 1 being the least important).

- Indicate which company need on their side would be satisfied by a successful resolution of each issue. The five categories to be used here are 1) short-term financial (cash flow) 2) long-term financial (revenue growth and profits); 3) marketing (business image); 4) human resources (company morale); and 5) continued relations with outside vendors (external stability). More than one need may be listed.

Issue	Importance Value	Need(s)
1.		
2.		
3.		
4.		
5.		
6.		
7.		

Negotiation: Worksheet 12

Companies are made up of individuals who have complementary needs that must be satisfied. Incentive and reward systems in organizations recognize such needs; negotiation planning should recognize them as well. Individuals must feel they succeeded in a negotiation in their professional capacity, as well as feel that their company's needs have been met. Therefore, it is important to understand what motivates those that will be operating on the company's behalf. This worksheet analyzes the needs of each issue (ranked in order by importance value) for each negotiation participant on your side. The needs are categorized in descending order of importance: 1) survival; 2) safety; 3) belonging; 4) worth; and 5) self-actualization (the Maslow Triangle).

12. Analyzing Individual Needs: Your Side

- List the issues of the negotiation in order of importance and assign a value for each on a 1-10 scale (10 being the most important, 1 being the least important).

- Indicate those on your side who will be participating in the negotiation, in order of level of authority.

- For each issue and individual, indicate what personal needs will be satisfied through a successful resolution of the issue. The five categories to be used here are 1) survival; 2) safety; 3) belonging; 4) worth; and 5) self-actualization (Maslow Triangle). More than one need may be listed.

Issue	Importance Value	Negotiation Participant	Need(s)
1.			
2.			
3.			
4.			
5.			
6.			
7.			

Negotiation: Worksheet 13

This assessment should be repeated for their side, most likely after an initial meeting with them. Information from people inside your company may be useful in fleshing out personal motivations based upon prior contact with the other side's organization and/or its negotiation participants.

13. *Analyzing Individual Needs: Their Side*

- List the issues of negotiation in order of importance to their side, and assign a value for each on a 1-10 scale (10 being the most important, 1 being the least important).

- Indicate those on their side who are participating in the negotiation, in order of level of authority.

- For each issue and individual, indicate what personal needs will be satisfied through a successful resolution of the issue. The five categories to be used here are 1) survival; 2) safety; 3) belonging; 4) worth; and 5) self-actualization (the Maslow Triangle). More than one need may be listed.

Issue	Importance Value	Negotiation Participant	Need(s)

1.

2.

3.

4.

5.

6.

7.

Negotiation: Worksheet 14

Broadcast negotiations are creatures of the commercial marketplace. At the station level, managers must be aware of both national trends and local market conditions. Viewed broadly, transaction-oriented market conditions generally favor the buyer over the seller (or vice versa) at any particular time. Additionally, over the years, a larger pattern becomes established so that it is possible to predict with some certainty what market conditions cause the pendulum to swing back and forth, and when. This worksheet allows for the complication of current and historical market trend data at both the national and local levels, and for noting differences between past and present events.

14. Market Condition Analysis

- There is a relevant market for virtually every area that is subject to negotiation by broadcast managers. At the most general level, there is the national market. Are current conditions favorable to your side or theirs? How do current conditions compare to historical data about the marketplace? Do marketplace forces follow a pattern and, if so, what does that pattern show?

- Local marketplace conditions may or may not coincide with national trends. Thus, it is important to separately characterize the current local conditions as favorable to your side or theirs. Current local conditions also should be compared to historical data about the local marketplace to determine if there is a pattern, and if so, to articulate what that pattern shows.

National Market   **Current Conditions**   **Who Conditions Favor (You, Them)**

Local Market   **Current Conditions**   **Who Conditions Favor (You, Them)**

14. Market Condition Analysis *(continued)*

National Market **Description of Pattern, If Any**

Local Market History **Description of Pattern, If Any**

Differences Between Current National Conditions and Local Conditions **Reasons for Differences**

Negotiation: Worksheet 15

Negotiation strategies are long-range goals and values; negotiation tactics are operational maneuvers and techniques that are used to implement a strategy. As negotiation expert Chester L. Karrass notes, "Good strategy can be offset by poor tactics; good tactics can make the best of poor strategy. The effective negotiator is at home with both." Strategy is the more general concern, and as such, should be established at the outset. For example, is your strategy to charge premium rates or to "low ball"? Is it to pay the least amount of money or to pay the most in order to gain a competitive advantage? Always keep in mind that the choice of tactical options will be limited by the strategy you set. It will not be useful to violate a long-range goal solely to achieve a short-term gain. For each issue ranked in order by importance value, articulate what strategy you will be using and the tactics you will employ. Taken together, this worksheet will help you assess whether your overall strategy hangs together and whether your tactics are consistent with the strategy you have established.

15. Negotiation Strategies and Tactics: Your Side

- List each issue of the negotiation in order of importance and assign a value on a 1-10 scale (10 being the most important, 1 being the least important).

- Indicate for each issue what strategy your side will use to achieve a successful resolution. What is the overall plan?

- What tactics will be used to implement the strategy for resolving each issue? What specific activities will be undertaken?

Issue	Importance Value	Strategy	Tactics
1.			
2.			
3.			
4.			
5.			
6.			
7.			

Negotiation: Worksheet 16

This worksheet differs from the prior one by emphasizing tactics that are actually utilized by their side during negotiations. By focusing on tactical concerns, it is often possible to determine the overall strategy for each issue as well.

16. Negotiation Tactics and Strategies: Their Side

- List each issue of the negotiation introduced by their side and assign a value on a 1-10 scale (10 being the most important, 1 being the least important).

- Indicate the tactics that their side has employed to further each of its issues. What specific activities have been undertaken?

- Based on an evaluation of the tactics employed, can their side's strategy for advancing each issue be perceived? If so, indicate the perceived strategy in the appropriate space.

Issue	Importance Value	Tactics	Perceived Strategy
1.			
2.			
3.			
4.			
5.			
6.			
7.			

Negotiation: Worksheet 17

Negotiation expert Gerard I. Nierenberg has developed a comprehensive analysis of the role that questions play in negotiation. According to him, "asking questions is an effective way to uncover your opposer's thoughts and to assist him in the formation of his ideas. Questions permit you to channel the stream of conversation in any direction you may choose. . . . Asking a question is like sharpening a pencil: Each apt question helps to whittle down the problem."

It is useful to keep in mind Gerard Nierenberg's categorization of the five basic functions of questions. First, questions can be used to cause attention and provide preparatory conditions for substantive discussion. For example, "How are you?" Questions also can be used to obtain information, as in "How much is it?' They can provide information as well (e.g., "Did you know that . . .?). They can be used to stimulate thinking on the other side (e.g., "What would you suggest here?"). Finally, questions can be used to bring the other side's thinking to a conclusion, as in "Isn't it time we settle on these terms now?"

This worksheet should be utilized to prepare a list of questions that will be asked, and to prepare answers for questions that you anticipate will be raised by the other side.

17. Formulating Questions and Responses

Questions To Be Asked	To Whom
1.	
2.	
3.	
4.	
5.	
6.	
7.	

17. Formulating Questions and Responses *(continued)*

Anticipated Questions	Proposed Response	By Whom
1.		
2.		
3.		
4.		
5.		
6.		
7.		

Negotiation: Worksheet 18

Some of the worksheets already discussed, particularly those dealing with their side, can only be completed once negotiation meetings have begun. This is because an ongoing negotiation allows you to fill in details about their side based upon facts rather than on speculation. Whether worksheets are completed during pre-planning or at a later time, it is important to build in a re-evaluation stage to assess how closely your plans correspond to reality. This is best accomplished in the midst of the negotiation itself, when the stakes are highest and your impressions are immediate. Such an assessment also underscores the importance of being receptive to new information and flexible in modifying strategies and tactics to achieve a better outcome. This worksheet encourages a thorough review of what has transpired so far, with an eye toward making adjustments if necessary.

18. Assessing An Ongoing Negotiation

- Review the original issues lists from your side and their side. Are these issues still part of the negotiation? For those that are, have the order of importance and importance value changed for any issue on either side? For those that have not, have the issues been resolved to the satisfaction of both sides?

- If new issues have arisen on either side, what are they and what is their order of importance and importance value?

- Have any issues that either side sought to avoid become part of the negotiation? What effect have these issues had on other issues that are part of the negotiation?

- Have the company needs of either side changed since the negotiation began? If so, how?

- Are the participants in the negotiation or the level of authority on either side different than anticipated? If so, who are the new participants and what are their individual needs for each issue? What different levels of authority are now apparent?

- Have relevant marketplace conditions for either side changed since the negotiation began? If so, how?

- What changes in strategy and tactics have taken place on either side since the negotiation began?

Negotiation Issues/ Your Side	Importance Value	Issues Resolved	How Resolved
1.			
2.			
3.			
4.			
5.			
6.			
7.			

18. Assessing An Ongoing Negotiation *(continued)*

Negotiation Issues/ Their Side	Importance Value	Issues Resolved	How Resolved
1.			
2.			
3.			
4.			
5.			
6.			
7.			

Impact of New Issues on Old Ones:

18. Assessing An Ongoing Negotiation *(continued)*

Changes in Company Needs:

Negotiation Participants/ Your Side	Level of Authority	Individual Needs
1.		
2.		
3.		
4.		
5.		

Negotiation Participants/ Their Side	Level of Authority	Individual Needs
1.		
2.		
3.		
4.		
5.		

Worksheets

18. Assessing An Ongoing Negotiation *(continued)*

          Changes in
          Marketplace   Who Changes
          Conditions   Favor

1.

2.

3.

        Changes in Strategy   Changes in Tactics
        By Issue/Your Side   By Issue/Your Side

1.

2.

3.

        Changes in Strategy   Changes in Tactics
        By Issue/Their Side   By Issue/Their Side

1.

2.

3.

Negotiation: Worksheet 19

Perhaps the most overlooked phase in negotiation is post-negotiation review. There is a strong, yet understandable, tendency to move on to other matters once agreement has been reached. Similarly, if negotiation talks end, the tendency is to move on rather than dwell on something that may be perceived as a company-wide or personal failure. But in order to become a more effective negotiator over time, you should resist the temptation to leave everything you have learned and accomplished behind. Negotiation, like most other aspects of business, operates on a learning curve. The negotiation learning curve is one that lasts a lifetime, and any effort on your part to learn from past experiences will yield beneficial results in the future. What worked and what did not? Equally important, why did the outcome turn out as it did? Finally, what general lessons can be drawn for subsequent negotiations?

19. Reviewing A Negotiation Outcome

1. What issues on either side were not anticipated in advance?

2. Was the best response to exclude issues from the negotiation effective? If not, what would have been a better way to deal with these issues?

3. Were the appropriate participants part of the negotiation? If not, why weren't they present?

4. Did the negotiation proceed on the planned timetable? If not, was the actual timetable a more reasonable one to follow?

5. Was sufficient information available to support the resolution of each issue? If not, how can procedures be improved to gather better information?

6. Was the perception of the relevant marketplace correct? If not, what procedures can be implemented to obtain a more accurate picture of the marketplace?

7. Was the perception of company and individual needs accurate? If not, what procedures can be implemented to obtain a better assessment of these needs?

19. Reviewing A Negotiation Outcome *(continued)*

8. Which tactics were effective and which tactics were ineffective? Were the tactics useful to further strategic goals that had been established? If not, why?

9. What new options or alternatives were introduced during the negotiation?

10. How does the outcome affect your relationship with the other side?

11. What follow-up steps must be taken to implement the terms of the agreement reached during the negotiation?

12. Where issues were not resolved, or where the negotiation ended without a satisfactory resolution, what were the reasons that an agreement could not be reached? Was a lack of agreement beneficial or harmful to your business activities and the business activities of the other side?

13. When will another negotiation of this type arise? With whom?

14. Are there any refinements in the planning process or in actual negotiations that would be useful in improving the outcome of future, comparable negotiations?

Acknowledgements

Perhaps the single most important thought that I hope you carry away from this book is that negotiation is a collaborative process, one that requires constant feedback and cooperation. For me, this book has underscored the importance of collaboration in writing about negotiation planning, strategies and tactics as well.

Various staff and committee members of the NAB have provided a wealth of information and advice that is reflected in every section. The NAB's Research and Planning Department deserves great credit for its support from the earliest stages of conception to final publication. Specific thanks go to Rick Ducey, Senior Vice President, and Marcia De Sonne, Director of Technology Assessment, for their advice during the early planning of this project. Mark Fratrik, Director of Financial and Economic Research, contributed in many important ways as the manuscript moved through its final stages.

The NAB's Research Committee provided able oversight and useful suggestions that have been incorporated in many ways. David Parnigoni, Senior Vice President, Radio, and Dick Hollands, Senior Vice President, Television, and their respective staffs were outstanding resources who helped ensure that this book reflect practical concerns of radio and television managers. Susan Hill, Vice President, NAB Library and Information Services, steered me toward valuable industry research materials and deserves recognition.

Outside the NAB, numerous industry executives contributed great insight into the unique nature of broadcast negotiations. Much of their wisdom is embodied in the interviews that represent this book's core. Because these interviews were conducted on a not-for-attribution basis, I can only thank collectively all those who devoted time and energy to participating in them. As the saying goes, "They know who they are."

The project staff for this book included Neil Kotimsky of the Boston University School of Management and Professor Doranne Jung of the School of Mass Communication, College of Communication, Boston University. Both provided valuable research about historical and current trends in advertising sales, radio ratings, and the television syndication marketplace.

Christine Delanjian and Susan Delanjian-Hennessey provided superb support in preparing both interview transcripts and the final manuscript.

Special appreciation is extended to Professor Norman Marcus of the School of Broadcasting and Film, College of Communication, Boston University. Professor Marcus, a former broadcast executive who now serves as Director of Boston University's Broadcast Administration Program, oversaw the detailed interviews that give this book so much flavor. His extensive knowledge of broadcast management, great interpersonal skills and willingness to engage his interviewees deserve widespread recognition. Equally important, Norman was always there to bounce ideas against and to challenge my assumptions with a fine blend of grace and a sense of humor.

On the personal side, Gloria Z. Greenfield, my wife, and Daniel Greenfield Brotman, my son, have kept me on my toes and will continue to do so, no doubt. They leave me with a wishful thought: if broadcasters can negotiate anything, then perhaps husbands and fathers can, too.

Stuart N. Brotman
January 1988

The Author

Stuart N. Brotman is a Boston-based senior management adviser for domestic and international communications, information, and entertainment industry clients. He formerly served as Special Assistant to the Director of the National Telecommunications and Information Administration (NTIA) in Washington, DC.

He is active in conducting management training on negotiation planning, strategies and tactics for broadcast managers, and has served as a negotiation consultant on numerous radio and television transactions.

Mr. Brotman is the editor of *The Telecommunications Deregulation Sourcebook*, a reference volume covering broadcasting, cable television and new video media, and common carriers. He also has written over 100 articles on topical communications issues, and is listed in *Who's Who in Finance and Industry*.